Making Sense of Children's Drawings

Making Sense of Children's Drawings

Angela Anning and Kathy Ring

Open University Press

Open University Press
McGraw-Hill Education
McGraw-Hill House
Shoppenhangers Road
Maidenhead
Berkshire
England
SL6 2QL

email: enquiries@openup.co.uk
world wide web: www.openup.co.uk

and Two Penn Plaza, New York, NY 10121–2289, USA

First published 2004

A catalogue record of this book is available from the British Library

ISBN 0335 21265 4 (pb) 0335 21266 2 (hb)

Library of Congress Cataloging-in-Publication Data
CIP data applied for

Typeset by YHT Ltd
Printed in the UK by Bell & Bain Ltd, Glasgow

Dedications

For Richard, Vicky, Simon and Ben, with thanks from Angela for being excellent play fellows.

For my parents and sister, Barry, Jo and Liz and all the adults and children who have helped to educate me. Kathy.

Contents

List of figures

Preface

When a young child draws they are offering us a window into their own developing understanding of the world and their relationships to significant people, things and places around them. Drawings provide rich insights into young children's thinking and developing sense of self, including their gender roles. Drawing also provides children with a tool for telling themselves and us elaborate stories. However, what they draw and how they draw reflect the complexity of communication systems and visual images, signs and symbol systems in the domestic and leisure activities around them. They are encultured into using a wide range of graphicacy through their everyday experiences.

Many adults in both home and school contexts are unsure about how to respond to young children's drawings. Children's early attempts at making meaning in line may be dismissed as scribbling; and children soon hear the message that scribbling is associated with messiness and deviance – the defacing of pristine books and walls. Yet a parallel early meaning making in speech, babbling, is greeted with great enthusiasm by adults. When babbling, children gain positive feedback and reinforcement to babble on. Scribbling though is something not quite nice.

The adults and siblings in closest contact with young children shape babbling into speech sounds. A 'Ma Ma' becomes 'Mummy'. In a similar way, scribbling is shaped by well meaning adults and siblings into representations of people and objects. A circle with dots becomes a face with eyes. From then on, the message for children and those who respond to their drawings and draw with or for them is to make their representations of things look like things. As children enter an educational context, practitioners guide them towards the dual conventions of representational drawing and emergent writing. Children learn quickly that their own personal styles of drawing and their passions and preoccupations from home are not valued by their teachers. They enter the lettered world of school literacy where drawing assumes a secondary role to writing within the value systems of schooling.

The focus of this book is a powerful argument for the reappraisal of the role of drawing in young children's learning and in their attempts to make sense of and represent the worlds in which they are nurtured and educated. It draws on seven detailed case studies of children learning to draw and drawing to learn between the ages of 3 and 7 in the contexts of home and pre-school/school.

We know that it is important to listen carefully and respectfully to young children in order to be able to tune into their ideas, feelings, understandings and passions. We offer this text in the spirit of advocacy for the rights of young children to be taken seriously. We believe that children's drawing is under-valued, under-researched and misunderstood within the domains of childhood studies and early childhood education. We believe that drawing offers a powerful vehicle for hearing what young children are telling us. Shoehorning young children into narrow versions of drawing at school entry deprives them of a powerful mode of meaning making. Our hope is that this book will help others to stop, look and listen to their drawings and what they tell us about children's worlds.

Acknowledgements

Our thanks go to the children and parents involved in the study for their ongoing commitment and enthusiasm for the project and to the practitioners who spent time collating and reflecting upon children's drawings at a time when they were overly burdened with new government policy.

1 Young children making meaning at home and school

Introduction

Children's early mark making and drawing, which are the focus of this book, reflect the complexity of communication and sign systems in the communities where they are reared and educated. They also reflect the child's own feelings, interests, and sense of self and personal aesthetics.

Young children use a range of ways of communicating including facial expressions, gestures, body language, speech, socio-dramatic play, dancing, singing, manipulating objects, as well as mark making and drawing. They learn how to communicate in interactions with siblings or significant adults in the communities around them. In turn the nature and quality of these interactions are influenced by the historical and cultural contexts in which the interactions take place.

In this chapter we will explore:

- current theories about how children learn to communicate
- how children learn to make meanings and represent them in a range of modes including drawing
- how features of the contrasting socio-cultural contexts of home and pre-school/school in which they learn to draw impact on what and how they draw.

Learning to communicate

From birth the baby is a social being in his or her own right. Studies of infants and parents at home have shown how they 'tune into each other' through exchanging facial expressions (the first smile from a baby is a magic moment for both parent and baby), hand gestures (stroking and patting) and movements (such as head shaking and the joy of playing peek-a-boo, with all the attendant shared laughter) (Trevarthen 1995). These interactive rituals and games develop into 'proto-language' as the baby combines vocalizations, facial expressions and movements designed to retain the attention of their parent, carer or sibling.

It is not only people that matter to a baby. As Vygostky (1987) argued, things are also socially significant. All human actions, including thinking and speaking, involve the mediation of some kind of object as a sign or tool. So for example, a breast or bottle becomes both a sign of comfort and a tool for nurture. Later, as the infant becomes a sleepless toddler, the dual role of tool (a cup of water) and sign (Mummy is still caring for me) is reflected in that well known cry, 'Mummy, I want a drink'.

Schaffer (1992) called these interactions between adults and children around objects 'joint involvement episodes'. When an adult and a child pay joint attention to and act upon an object, it can provide both a source of emotional security and a tool for learning. At the early stages of adult/child interactions the object might be a cuddly toy; but later it may become something more abstract like the play with words aligned to the finger game of Round and Round the Garden. An important point is that these episodes are based on 'everyday' exchanges and that wherever they occur – in home or day-care contexts – the quality of interactions around the objects is critical to the quality of the child's learning (Anning and Edwards 1999). A second important point is that it is often the child who takes the lead in these dyadic interactions.

It is in the context of the child's own interests that the adult can then introduce additional material, for example, a verbal label for the object the child has just picked up or an extension of the verbalization the child has just uttered (Schaffer 1996: 253).

The same object may be used in contrasting ways in the different contexts in which young children learn to communicate. For example, at home a storybook may be used as a source of comfort and reassurance for the intimate one to one ritual of a bedtime story by their parent. When they attend a preschool playgroup, children may observe that same storybook being used by a playgroup worker as a tool to keep a large group of children sitting still on the carpet whilst the rest of the team tidy away the equipment at the end of a play session.

In this book we are concerned particularly to explore the interactions of young children with siblings and significant adults in their home and preschool/school contexts around objects for mark making and drawing: scraps of paper, easels, megasketchers and felt tips, crayons, chalks and pencils.

Learning to make meanings and to represent them

Children in the so-called developed world are bombarded with visual information from the media. Some images are moving, as in television programmes and advertisements, videos and computer games. Some images are static, as on street and shop signs, advertisements on hoardings, catalogues, magazines and books (though some of these now include moving images in pop up or interactive formats). Young children learn to decode these visual images in 'joint involvement episodes' alongside the more experienced users of these images in their families and within the communities where they live out their daily lives. Children draw on these visual resources and models offered by more experienced members of their communities of how to represent things, when they begin to make and represent meanings for themselves.

Kress (1997) made an influential study of his own young children's journeys into meaning making. He observed and recorded episodes of his children engaged in multi-modal representations using:

- found materials to make models
- household furniture and objects mingled with toys to make 'worlds' in which to act out involved narratives in play episodes
- mark making media such as felt tips and paint to 'draw' elaborate versions of their understanding of the world around them.

He argues that 'children act multi-modally, both in the things they use, the objects they make, and in the engagement of their bodies; there is no separation of body and mind' (Kress 1997: 97). He calls their representations 'the energetic, interested, intentional action of children in their effects on their world' (Kress: 114). He also draws attention to the dynamic interrelation between what resources (such as discarded boxes, glue, paper, felt tips, small play figures) are available to children for making representations and the child's 'shifting interest' and their ability to move creatively from one mode to another. For example, he observed his children using scissors to cut out their drawn representations, or to cut out images from discarded greeting cards, and using the cut out objects as three-dimensional play things in elaborate socio-dramatic play bouts. The cut out objects bridged the gap between the two- and three-dimensional world for the children. He sees young children's play-based narratives as 'hybrid things with language used to indicate action and narrative sequence, and drawing used to represent, to display, the people and objects in the story' (Kress 1997: 24). His insightful analysis of the observations of his children at play allows us to marvel at young children's flexibility of thinking and their unselfconscious ability to flick from one mode of representation to another. These are capabilities that many artists spend their working lives trying to recapture.

Pahl (1999, 2002) is one of the few UK-based researchers to have observed, with equal sensitivity and attention to detail as Kress in his home-based studies, the meaning making of young children in a nursery class. She recorded episodes of children creating layers of narrative as they represented and re-represented versions of stories in their socio-dramatic play. Objects were used with a 'fluid quality'. A shopping basket made from a cereal packet and strips of card for role-play in the nursery might be transformed into a carrycot for a doll cut out from a shopping catalogue and carried home at the end of the nursery session. She sees these experiments in representation and meaning making as opportunities for children to explore what is 'me' and 'not me', using the models they create as 'transactional objects'.

Pahl's observations of young children engaged in socio-dramatic play reflect Vygotsky's (1995) argument that for children there is a close relationship between narrative, art and play. Linqvist (2001) comments:

> Vygotsky argues that children's creativity in its original form is syncretistic creativity, which means that the individual arts have yet to be separated and specialized. Children do not differentiate between poetry and prose, narration and drama. Children draw pictures and tell a story at the same time; they act a role and create their lines as they go along. Children rarely spend a long time completing each creation, but produce something in an instant, focusing all their emotions on what they are doing at that moment in time.
>
> (Lindqvist 2001:8)

Dyson (1993a), a researcher based in the USA, is a third influential observer of young children's meaning making and representations. She argues that making symbols is 'the essence of being human' and that drawing, as one of the symbol systems at our disposal, is one way for humans to liberate ourselves from the 'here and now'. Figure 1.1 draws on Dyson's model. The model situates the development of drawing as both a sequential and

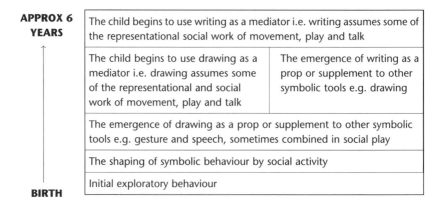

Figure 1.1 The situated nature of drawing within a continuum of children's use of symbol systems (developed from Dyson 1993a)

cumulative process. It also highlights the significance of the interrelationship between gesture, speech, play, drawing and writing for the young child.

There has been some research into the relationship between the development of writing and drawing in studies of emergent literacy (for example: Bissex 1980; Hall 1987; Dyson 1989; Kress 1997). Dyson's argument is that at around the age of 2 children begin to use drawing as an additional prop for story telling in socio-dramatic play, with others or alone, to complement the 'old, comfortable procedures' of dramatic gesture and speech. As they begin to experiment with making letter shapes, they make no distinction between drawing and writing. They use the two modes in parallel in a process of 'symbol weaving' as they begin to 'write' stories (Dyson 1986). She claims that making distinctions for children too early, between drawing and writing, detracts from young children's ability to compose stories (Dyson 1993a). We will pursue this argument later in the book.

We are becoming increasingly aware that the organizational tool of narrative for learning has been under-rated in research into young children's cognitive development. Egan (1989) has long been an advocate of the story form as a cultural universal which 'reflects a basic and powerful form in which we makes sense of the world and experience' (p. 2). Young children's personal narratives offer tools for them to order and explain the complexity of their experiences of the world. Gallas (1994: xv) describes these narratives as 'part of the silent language that embodies thinking'. The narratives may be expressed in dramatic play, movement, song, speech, drawings and paintings.

Socio-cultural theory

Within the domain of what is called socio-cultural theory, there is growing interest in the effect of the cultural context on how children learn (for example see Rogoff 1990; Lave and Wenger 1991). We know that children pick up on cues from siblings, peers and significant adults in their everyday lives about what are 'appropriate' learning behaviours. A clear example of the impact of the context on learning behaviours is that before children enter educational contexts, they are the main initiators of questions. Anyone who has spent time with a lively 3-year-old knows how exhausting answering those *why* questions can be! As the child makes the transition into being a pupil in a pre-school setting, they discover that within the rules of educational discourse, suddenly it is the adults who ask all the questions. What is even more bizarre is that the answers to the adults' questions are often perceived by the child to be inconsequential or downright obvious: 'What colour are your shoes today?' 'How many teddies are in the bed?' 'What shape is this biscuit?'

Such shifts in expectations of 'appropriate' learning behaviours in different contexts impact on children's developing sense of self – who they are and what they are expected to become – and on what they feel they can and should do. Their developing sense of themselves as learners affects their motivation, or what has been called their 'disposition' to learn. So if someone at home has encouraged the child to draw, supporting them in problem solving with a sense of enjoyment and fun but without putting them under pressure, and modelled persistence in activities that are unfamiliar, the child is likely to take a positive disposition to drawing activities when they enter pre-school or school contexts. We call this developing a 'mastery' orientation to learning (Dweck 1991). The opposite, a 'helpless' orientation to tackling tasks can result from an adult in the new setting undermining the child's confidence in their drawing ability by responding negatively to their familiar drawing behaviours, or by over-correction or insensitive shaping of the child's drawings into narrow 'school' versions of representations.

Young children have to make sense of the continuities and discontinuities between their experiences of different kinds of tools (such as the distinctive styles of language used by adults at home and in school), objects or artefacts (such as colouring books from the supermarket and number activity worksheets in a nursery class) and activities (such as making a birthday card for Grandma at home or drawing an apple from observation in an Early Years Unit based art lesson). Figure 1.2 depicts these sometimes complementary but often contrasting influences in home and school contexts on the child's learning behaviours and meaning making.

Home influences on children's meaning making

For young children at home, the rites and rituals of family life are expressions of particular family histories and their cultural heritages, the preoccupations of adults and the impact of popular culture. These three factors influence the roles and responsibilities taken by adults (main breadwinner, child carer), by children (the baby of the family, the clever one) and by significant others (reliable grandma, occasional father) within the household. Family histories will also impact on the kinds of activities seen as the 'norm' at home such as Sunday lunches around a table, television snack teas on trays, going to church on Sundays, watching *Eastenders* together. The kind of objects around the house will reflect family choices of activities: comfortable furniture in the living room, family photographs on the television, a heap of discarded papers and biros on the kitchen table. Where objects are kept will reflect contructs of what is deemed to be important for the adults and what for the children: Dad's motorbike in the hall, a doll's house upstairs in Jenny's bedroom and a Meccano set in her brother Tom's.

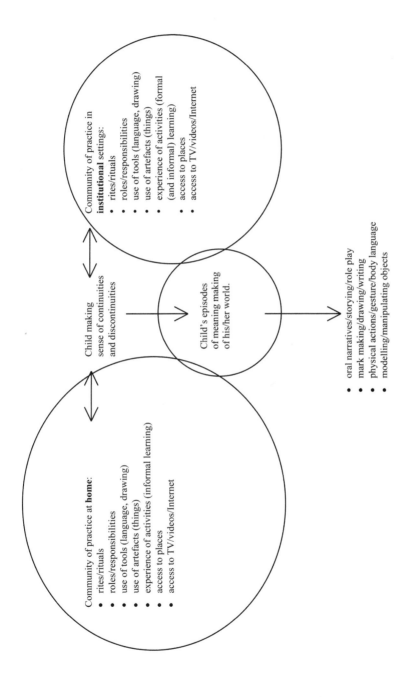

Figure 1.2 Home and school influences on a child's meaning making

Pahl's (2002) ethnographic study of three boys aged between 5 and 8 at home revealed the way space was contested between the boys and their parents on 'the cusp of mess and tidiness' (Pahl 2002: 147). Children's meaning making moves between bedroom floor to living room floor, taking in materials as diverse as prayer beads, paper, glue, modelling, material and card. The children drew on cultural resources around them, including stories and narratives.

Pahl is an advocate for children to be given space for purposeful mess in homes without constantly being nagged to tidy up. She argues that the advantage for children of meaning making at home is the opportunities they have to move fluidly from one activity to another, often without the watchful gaze of adults. Home should be a place where children and adults are able to weave in and out of each other's spaces.

One significant shared space for families is around the television. Marsh (2002) points out that media texts, from television, videos and computer games, provide a shared resource from which to make meaning for parents and children. She investigated the media use of 26 children between 2 years 6 months and 3 years 11 months as a follow up to a survey of a large sample of parents within a Sure Start programme area in a northern city in the UK. Sure Start is a massive government anti-poverty initiative aimed at young children and their families. She observed that the children regularly played out narratives based on what they had seen on television with the implicit support of their parents.

> In many of the homes visited, the space around the television appeared to be demarcated as a space for celebrating and extending children's relationship with the screen. Often, children's dressing-up clothes, toys or books which were associated with television characters were situated there, ready to be taken up by the children when necessary.
>
> (Marsh 2002: 6)

In the homes there was plenty of evidence of the children's popular culture in such diverse artefacts as stickers, comics, games, toys, clothing, cards, jewellery, sports accessories, jokes, jingles, and even food and drink. Amongst these generalized, commercially produced, cultural artefacts children had preferences for and affiliations with specific images and objects. These preferences were often gendered.

It is to be expected that young children's sense of self be strongly influenced by their view of themselves as boy or girl. From birth children are labelled within society on the basis of their gender. Bailey (1993) summarizes a collection of research evidence as:

Studies show that socialization into appropriate gender roles begins at birth as girls, wrapped in pink blankets, are treated quietly, talked to softly, and described as being dainty, gentle, quiet and cuddly, while boys are dressed in blue, referred to in terms of being big, strong and athletic, and handled in a more aggressive, playful manner.

(Bailey 1993: 117)

The gender values and beliefs of adults, siblings and friends with whom they come in contact have an overwhelming impact on young children's own beliefs. Stereotyping within imagery from mass media and from the marketing of toys, clothes, activities and equipment for boys and girls reinforces these strong messages about the 'correct' way to be a boy or girl. These beliefs are reflected in the content and styles of boy and girl play, representations and drawings; but little research has been published into the gendered nature of children's drawings. Exceptions are the work of Golumb and Dyson.

Golumb (1992) drew on detailed, longitudinal studies of gifted children; for example, the horse drawings of Heidi between the ages of 3 and 10 (Fein 1984) and the space world drawings of Roger between the ages of 6 and 13 (Blake 1988). She summarizes her findings:

...the spontaneous productions of boys reveal an intense concern with warfare, actions of violence and destruction, machinery and sports contests, whereas girls depict more tranquil scenes of romance, family life, landscapes and children at play.

(Golomb 1992: 158)

Dyson (1986) collected the free drawings of children attending a kindergarten over a 5-month period and recorded their dictations and talk as they drew. Overall boys chose to depict 'explosions, battles, and displays of power and motion' with actors and actions moving through time accompanied by dramatizing actions and related speech. Girls chose to draw 'happy little girls and cheerful small animals'. For example, of one girl Dyson wrote, 'As she talked and drew their hair and clothes, one might think she was dressing her dolls, rather than drawing her girl' (Dyson 1986: 393). We suspect that a contemporary study of children's free drawings would reveal far more influence of media imagery.

Of course, the reactions of parents to young children's drawings are also important. Malchiodi (1998), an art therapist, points out:

Remarks made by a parent can have an impact on children's desire and motivation to make art; even the most well-meaning parent has, on occasion, misinterpreted the content of a child's drawing, perhaps unknowingly discouraging the child from continuing to draw.

(Malchiodi 1998: 22)

She echoes Schaffer's argument about the importance of parents being able to 'tune into' their children's preoccupations in general, but also specifically in relation to drawing as a window into their children's social and emotional states.

Matthews (1994), a practising artist himself, is a passionate advocate of parents' roles in encouraging their children to be confident drawers. He sees their role as partly to provide the kind of environment where children have the physical and mental space and resources to explore painting, drawing and model making. But of equal importance is for parents to provide a place 'where children feel confident that people will take their drawings seriously, and where it would be unheard of for a child's drawing to be dismissed as mere scribbling' (Matthews 1994: 124). Matthew's seminal, longitudinal studies of his own three children's drawing development provide powerful insights into the intentional nature of all young children's mark making and drawings and the impact of parents as partners in supporting their children's creativity.

School influences on children's meaning making

Just as family histories affect the everyday lives of young children at home, so the legacies and ideologies from the history of art education affect their lived experiences of learning to draw in educational settings (Anning 1995, 1997b). When elementary schools were established for the children of the working classes in the nineteenth century, art was seen as servicing the development of 'skill of hand and eye' to ensure that the nation was training a useful and productive industrial workforce. Art lessons consisted of copying pictures chalked up on the blackboard by the teacher or from instructional books, learning how to draw three-dimensional shapes and structured tasks in colour identification and pattern making (Tomlinson 1947).

Frank Cizek's pioneering work on child art in the 1930s persuaded educationalists that children's artwork had integrity in its own right. Much like the approach to promoting creativity articulated in the influential exhibition, The Hundred Languages of Children, of the Reggio Emilia pre-school programme in our time, Cizek's principles were disseminated through travelling exhibitions of child art. His approach was promoted by Marion Richardson in the UK. Richardson's approach to art education for children was quite structured. She recommended simple exercises such as pattern making using vivid materials such as powder paints and thick brushes. Yet adults were urged not to impose their techniques and aesthetic standards on children and not to 'interfere' with children's creative, spontaneous expressions in line and paint. It was enough just to set out materials for them and leave them to explore their possibilities and 'blossom'. Influential theories about developmental stages in children's drawing such as Kellogg's (1969) compounded such beliefs. She wrote: 'In terms of spontaneous art, every child is a "born artist" who should be allowed to scribble without oppressive guidance in art education' (Kellogg 1969: 266). Arguments for 'free expression' in art education gathered force within the general shift towards 'progressivism' (Abbs 1987).

Herbert Read (1943), Alec Clegg (1980) and Robin Tanner (1989) each in turn promoted the importance of aesthetic and creative aspects of the curriculum. In the 1960s, when progressivism was the zeitgeist, the seminal report on primary education, the Plowden Report (CACE 1967) encapsulated the spirit of the times. Of art the authors wrote: 'Art is both a form of communication and a means of expression of feelings which ought to permeate the whole curriculum and the whole life of the school' (CACE 1967: 247). In fact, as with many aspects of progressivism, the reality in classrooms rarely lived up to the rhetoric of the progressive movement. In primary schools, art was often used as a servicing agent for 'topic work': for example, decorating covers with felt tip pens for project folders about the planets or making models out of cardboard of Viking long ships following a history lesson.

For young children in infant classrooms art activities were set up and introduced by the class teacher at the beginning of the school day, but if the activities were supervised at all, it was often by a volunteer parent or a nursery nurse. In nursery classes, art activities were part of a routine, daily diet of activities for all the children: an easel set up for painting in the corner, or a mark making table for children to explore media and their own ideas. In addition, children would be called across to a table usually by a nursery nurse, to complete an adult directed set task. The tasks were generally related to topics and seasonal, such as painting snowdrops in spring, printing from autumn leaves in autumn or making set piece greetings cards to take home for Easter, Mother's Day or Christmas. Meanwhile in both infant and nursery classes teachers tended to position themselves at the 'work' tables in the centre of the classrooms to supervise the 'status' activities related to literacy and numeracy. It was made quite clear to children which were the 'important' activities.

Teachers were exhorted to showcase the 'best' artwork on the ever-growing acreage of display boards in primary schools. Displays assumed the role of 'window dressing' in an educational climate which encouraged parents to use choice of schools in a free market economy to 'weed out' unsuccessful schools for closure. At worst feeding the display imperative resulted in children spending hours aimlessly sticking small squares of fabric or screwed up tissue paper onto adult drawn outlines of bunnies (in spring), the seaside (in summer), harvest fayre (in autumn) and snowmen (in winter).

Inevitably the dominance of 'free expression' in arts education began to be questioned. For example, in the USA Elliott Eisner challenged the notion that development in art was simply about maturation and the unfolding of natural talents. He argued that the creation and appreciation of art 'is not an automatic consequence of maturation, but rather a process that is affected by the type of experience children have had' and that 'a child's ability is a function of what he (sic) has learned' (Eisner 1972: 105). In the UK this argument was reflected in the influential Gulbenkian Report: 'The task is not simply to let anything happen in the name of self-expression or creativity. Neither is it to impose rigid structures or ideas and methods upon the children. The need is for a difficult balance of freedom and authority' (Robinson 1982: 33).

It was at this historical, cultural time in 1988 that a National Curriculum was introduced in the UK. Statutory Orders for a Key Stage One Art Curriculum, for children aged between 5 and 7, were delivered in primary schools from September 1992. Predictably, given their low status in the educational system, art and music, with physical education, were the last National Curriculum subjects to be introduced into schools. There were two Attainment Targets in the Art Orders: Investigating and Making; and Knowledge and Understanding.

Primary teachers were ill-prepared to deliver the art curriculum. A study by Cleave and Sharp in 1986 found that most Post-Graduate Certificate in Education (PGCE) primary initial teacher training courses included only 20 hours designated to teaching art, and Bachelor of Education (BEd) courses between 12 and 40 hours (Cleave and Sharp 1986). Not surprisingly, when Clement (1993) surveyed 936 primary teachers' perspectives on delivering the new art curriculum, though they welcomed it in principle, in practice they felt ill-trained and lacking in confidence in its delivery.

Despite their misgivings, most primary teachers responded well to the demands of teaching the practical aspects of the art curriculum. Office for Standards in Education (Ofsted) annual reports on the quality of teaching and learning in primary schools reported steady improvements in the teaching of skills in making art across a broader range of two-dimensional media, though three-dimensional work remained under-developed. However, in the underpinning knowledge and understanding strand of the art curriculum, teachers' lack of confidence resulted in them offering children a restricted range of artists and designers to study. Lots of children's painted versions of Impressionist paintings were often copied from postcards on their desks. Children's copies of Monet's water lilies and Van Gogh's sunflowers, for example, replaced screwed up tissue paper friezes on primary school display boards.

Matthews has consistently argued that because the National Curriculum was based on the 'transmission or "delivery" of [these] bodies of knowledge to passive recipients, it is inevitably insensitive to children's development'

(Matthews 2001: 29). For him the prescribed curriculum has led to children's art 'having to fulfil an educational purpose of a particularly limited kind' and to 'an encouragement of overt teaching involving an active interference, on the part of teachers, with children's development' leading to 'the systematic devaluing of children's spontaneous art'. Though Matthews makes it clear that he does not want a return to the 'romantic', laissez-faire approach of the 1960s, nor does he want children's artistic development to be constrained as 'supposed deficits in need of correction until the form of representation socially sanctioned by society ... is reached' (Matthews 2003: 75).

When a labour government swept into power in 1997, the new Prime Minister Tony Blair's mantra was 'Education. Education. Education'. The government's concern to raise standards in literacy and numeracy in primary education drove educational reforms. A Literacy Hour was introduced in 1999 and a Numeracy Hour in 2000. Schools were set targets for testing children in Standard Assessment Tasks (SATs) at 7 and 11. Results were published in league tables in local and national newspapers. The content of SATs reflected the literacy and numeracy strategy targets rather than the National Curriculum. Educational discourse was dominated by the language of targets, tests, attainment, competence, appraisal, inspection, accountability, and failing schools. In such a climate hard won gains in art education in primary schools began to be eroded. Art was allocated less and less time in the primary school timetable.

From 2000 the Qualifications and Curriculum Authority (QCA), in an attempt to support schools in maintaining a broad and balanced curriculum, introduced subject-based schemes of work. When art was scheduled, hard-pressed teachers often relied on 'one off' lessons taken off the shelf from the QCA schemes of work. Children had few opportunities to pursue personal interests or styles in school art activities, including drawing. Teachers were told that 'children should practise their drawing skills on a regular basis' (QCA/DfEE 2000a: 4), but the exemplars given were restricted to observational drawing. Hamblin (2002) summarizes the depressing scenario of children's lived experiences of art lessons as:

> Creativity must be expressed in specific time increments (one hour or less), noise must be kept to a minimum, work produced must not be messy, the clean-up of materials must be accomplished in approximately five minutes, work spaces are depersonalized, and the products must be easily stored.
>
> (Hamblin 2002: 22)

A growing concern that young children, particularly boys, were suffering from 'too formal too soon' approaches to education (Sylva 1994; Anning 1997a) and consequently developing negative dispositions to learning, led to a significant initiative from the government in relation to the education of young children. In 2000 a Foundation Stage curriculum was introduced for all children aged from 3 to 5, including those in the Reception classes of primary schools, before they began the National Curriculum Key Stage One. The Foundation Stage guidance (QCA/DfEE 2000b) promotes the principles of children being educated across six areas of learning: personal, social and emotional; language and literacy; mathematics; knowledge and understanding of the world; physical development; creative development. However, the associated end of Foundation Stage statutory baseline assessment, before children begin Key Stage One, tests only the first three areas, that is, excluding science, the humanities, the arts and physical development.

The Standards agenda to improve literacy and numeracy attainments meant that creativity was neglected in all phases of statutory education, not just those catering for young children. Concerns were addressed that the narrowing of the curriculum was alienating many children at school, in particular disaffected and troublesome boys. In 2001 a committee (NACCCE 2001) reported on the importance of creativity in the school curriculum both for catering for the needs of a wide range of pupils but also as a marketable commodity. The report was followed up by a QCA led working party to investigate how the principles of the National Advisory Committee for Creative and Cultural Education (NACCCE) report might be translated into the National Curriculum framework.

Although these initiatives raise our hopes that more attention may be paid to the arts and creativity in the education of young children we still have much to fight for. The dominant messages for young children in primary schools remain that drawing is a low status, time-filling occupation; for example to while away the time in illustrating their written versions of stories, or to keep them quiet during wet play times. In art lessons, drawing is about observing and recording objects, such as flowers, fruits and museum artefacts – not things guaranteed to be of interest to lively young children! The main message is that in their drawings they must make things look as 'real' as possible. Peer pressure builds for drawings to conform to representational modes and children who have an ability to draw well quickly gain recognition amongst their peers. Those who find drawing difficult are offered little or no tuition to help them to improve their efforts. They quickly learn how to avoid drawing or to stick to well tried and tested stick figures, stylized houses and lollipop trees. Many adults continue to draw in this arrested, formulaic style.

In the context of pre-school settings, though children are given more freedom to explore their own agendas in the mark making areas of classrooms, constructive feedback from the adults is rare. If they carry their drawing across to show them to a busy teacher they may at best be rewarded with a vague, 'Lovely' or 'Mmm, what is it?' Their teachers are much more interested in whether they can write their name on the drawing.

But there is far more to young children's drawing than these messages imply. In Chapter 2 we will look more closely at what we know about young children learning to draw and drawing to learn.

2 Young children learning to draw

Definitions of drawing

Why do people draw? It may be because they want to use drawing as one of the modes available to them for exploring ideas. An architect might play with line to explore shapes and forms around a key concept from which may emerge the beginnings of ideas for the design of a building. A writer might doodle on a blank page to focus her mind on how she may tackle the next twist in the narrative. A child might scrawl zigzags in paint to represent his memory of a fast moving fairground ride. These kinds of drawings are defined by Perry (1992) as 'creative'. The activity of creative drawing, as in play, is often characterized by being in what Csiksentmihalyi (1979) described as a 'flow' state.

Yet when most of us think about a drawing, our concept is of what Perry calls 'representational' drawing. Representational drawings may also take many forms. A fashion designer might use the stylized conventions of drawing a mannequin to sketch a new outfit. An animator might meticulously work up a computer driven image of a monster for a children's cartoon series. A landscape artist may make several sketches of a view to use as a stimulus for decisions about how to frame her watercolour painting. Unlike creative drawings, representational drawings use traditional and well-rehearsed conventions of drawing modelled within the visual cultures in which they are generated. Both types of drawings may be executed in a wide range of media: for example, pencil and paper, paint and wall, mouse and screen, finger and chocolate sauce.

More importantly perhaps, for the aim of this book, are the questions of why many people do not choose to draw; or feel terrified when they are asked to do so; or are arrested in their ability to draw at the level of competence they had at 8 or 9 years of age. How could we contemplate such attitudes amongst the general population if we were asking the same questions about people and writing?

In order to try to answer these questions we need to take a look at the way scholars and researchers have tried to understand and explain both how children learn to draw and how they use drawing as a way of learning.

Research into children's drawing

Until the twentieth century interest in children's drawing was limited to a few enthusiasts, often parents or teachers, who kept collections of drawings from 'exceptional' children. Then two sources of interest generated scholarship and research into children's drawing. The first source was an exponential growth in the field of developmental psychology. The second was the radical rethinking of 'modern' art in the Western world in all its manifestations and its relationship to what was defined as 'primitive' art and to young children's art.

Developmental stages in drawing

The paradigm of developmental stages, argued through literature on the education of young children from Rousseau to Froebel, and above all through the seminal work of Piaget, filtered into early research into the development of drawing. Some of the research was based on longitudinal studies of individual children – often the researcher's own. One such influential study was published in France by Lucquet (1913, 1923). His work was based on observations of his daughter, Simone, who between the ages of 3 and 9 was encouraged to draw at the corner of her father's desk as he worked, and studies of drawings of the mentally ill. Lucquet classified the first stage as the 'scribbling' stage (for approximately 2- to 4-year-olds). At first the marks were random and purposeless, but through 'fortuitous realism' the child would suddenly discover 'meanings' in their scribbles. For example a circle would suggest a face. He defined the second stage (for 4- to 7-year-olds) as 'pre-schematic' when children's drawings were characterized by 'failed realism'. At the third stage, 'schematic' (for 7- to 9-year-olds) children were in the transitional stage between the idiosyncratic 'visually unrealistic' features of the second stage and the final and fourth stage (for 9- to 10 plus-year-olds) termed 'visual realism' when they were able to achieve 'realistic' representations of objects. Lucquet's work influenced many generations of researchers in the field.

Stage Theories informed the design in the 1920s of intelligence tests based on the notion of generalized, fixed sequences in children's development, such as Burt's IQ tests (Burt 1921) and Goodenough's Draw a Man Test (Goodenough 1926). Goodenough's test was based on the idea that the more complete and realistic the figure of a man drawn by the child, the higher they scored in intellectual maturity. She constructed age norms against levels of competence in drawing a man.

Lowenfeld (1947), an Austrian-American art educator rather than a psychologist, built on the Stage Theory idea that development was a journey towards an adult version of representation. His work was later updated in an influential text by Lowenfeld and Brittain (1982). He identified six stages of artistic development: scribbling (ages 2 to 4 years); pre-schematic (ages 4 to 7 years); schematic (ages 7 to 9 years); dawning realism (ages 9 to 11 years); pseudorealism (ages 11 to 13 years); and period of decision (adolescence). But Lowenfeld's interest in art education encouraged him to investigate individual differences in children's art as well as general stages. He saw art as a vehicle for the release of feelings and sensibilities. He identified two expressive styles in children's drawings: visual (reflecting the appearance of an object) and haptic (reflecting the most characteristic features of an object). He argued that spontaneous expressions of art from young children should never be 'interfered with' by teachers.

Other researchers collected large samples of children's drawings in what we call cross sectional studies, and used them to generalize about universal stages of drawing. Kellogg's (1969) work, referred to in Chapter 1, is probably the best known of these studies. She identified and classified 20 basic scribble types that formed the basis of all later graphical expressions. Scribble types ranged from dots, to horizontal and vertical lines, open and enclosed lines, loops, spirals to circles. She also investigated the way children placed their marks on paper and the sequences in which they made their drawings. Golomb (1981, 1992) later simplified Kellogg's complex model to two types of scribbles: loops and circles (generated by children's circular hand and arm movements) and parallel lines (generated by their horizontal, vertical or diagonal movements). The point about studies of large samples of drawings is that researchers were studying children's drawings disembedded from any consideration of children's intentions or of the contexts in which children were drawing. A second important point is that the research was dominated by the cognitive aspects of children's development in drawing. Few concessions were made to the affective, aesthetic and pyscho-motor aspects of development.

However, for us the key overarching concept in Stage Theories is that children's drawings were seen as 'deficit' as they worked towards the goal of visual realism. This construct of the purpose of drawing as portraying an accurate representation of objects, places and people was deeply entrenched in the traditions of fine art training in the Western world. Drawing naked bodies from life (life classes), observing and copying from iconic objects (casts of classical statuary), still lives (drawing fruit, household objects and stuffed animals) and, more daringly, studies of moving objects from nature (water, skies or animals in movement) were at the core of classical, fine art education. But for many cultures, for example the craft-based decoration of household objects in African art, the symbols-based recording of landscapes in Australian Aboriginal 'dream time' drawings, or the strict, decorative conventions of

Islamic religious life, there is no such tyranny of representation as the highest goal of artistry.

The child as artist

As long as children's art was perceived as a deficit version of adult art, it was unlikely to be taken seriously in its own right. It was the influence of a Viennese art educator, together with trends towards Expressionism in modern art, that were the catalysts for change.

At the turn of the century Frank Cizek, referred to in Chapter 1, was pursuing an interest in children's art inspired by children's drawing and painting classes in Vienna. Cizek promoted the idea that children's spontaneous artwork should be recognized as aesthetically pleasing in its own right and would lead seamlessly to creativity in adulthood. He argued that adults should not interfere with children's artwork to try to coax them into adult versions of representation (Viola 1936). He worked closely with Viennese artists and architects of the period – the best known of them is Gustav Klimt – who were enchanted by the children's artwork and turned to them, alongside the influences of art from many other cultures and periods, as visual stimuli. Viola reported, 'Some went as far as to say that these were the foundations of the new art education. Why go back to the Chinese, Japanese, ancient Egyptians, Babylonians, and Negroes (sic)? Here was that which they sought' (Viola 1936: 12–13).

It was left to art educators and art therapists, sometimes working within the disciplines of cognitive or clinical psychology, to focus on the affective and aesthetic aspects of children's drawings. Herbert Read (1943) argued passionately that the status of the aesthetic and creative should be raised in the school curriculum. As were many scholars of this period, he was influenced by the psychoanalytical theories of Freud and Jung about the role of the subconscious in people's thinking and behaviours. He focused clearly on the emotional and expressive content of children's drawings. He developed stylistic criteria for classifying children's artwork based on Jungian categories of introversion and extroversion. Generations of charismatic educators, such as Robin Tanner (1989) working from a base in Oxfordshire and Alec Clegg (1980) from the West Riding of Yorkshire, built on Read's work. Children's artwork from these sources is stunning. Yet a 'house style' is discernible in them. For example, there are still discernible legacies of the West Riding style in the artwork displayed in schools in pockets of Leeds and Doncaster. The artwork from Reggio Emilia also has a distinctive 'house style'. There is an inevitability that the influence of charismatic educationalists and their history and cultural assumptions has impacted on both the processes and products of children's art in these contexts. The question must be raised though of how much the children's own sense of personal aesthetics and their real abiding interests are represented in these fabulous but institutionally generated drawings and paintings.

It was an American philosopher, Nelson Goodman, who steered the study of children's art in another direction. In his seminal work, *Languages of Art* (Goodman 1976), he identified distinct symbolic systems embedded in the domains of language, gesture, music and visual arts. He argued that each has a symbol system in its own right. In 1967 he founded Project Zero at Harvard University. Research from this project promoted the significance of children's access to and mastery of symbol systems embedded in the cultures of domains of knowledge. The evidence accumulated of children's enculturation into these symbols by formal (educational) and informal (home/leisure) learning opportunities. Of the Harvard-based researchers Howard Gardner's work has been the most influential on early childhood education. His early work focused on developmental issues in children's acquisition of symbol systems, including the development of drawing (Gardner 1980). In later research he became preoccupied with understanding the relationship between the acquisition and mastery of symbol systems and different aspects of cognitive processing. This led to his influential Theory of Multiple Intelligences: 'seven different sets of "know how" identified as linguistic, musical, logical mathematical, spatial, bodily-kinesthetic, intrapersonal and interpersonal' (Davis and Gardner 1992: 102–3). Gardner argues that educational systems are dominated by promoting achievements in linguistic and logical mathematical intelligences and that for a genuinely 'all round' education we need to plan a curriculum based on all seven aspects of intelligence.

In the late 1960s within the field of psychology, particularly in the USA, there was a shift in interest to gestalt theories. Drawing on gestalt theories, Arnheim (1969) investigated graphic development as a cognitive process. He was interested both in the processes of perception and representation as cognitive acts. He argued that in learning to look the child must actively select, abstract and generalize from aspects of what they perceive. Arnheim believed that visual images 'spoke' directly to an observer. It was not necessary to have the mediation of explanations in words for them to make sense. This holistic approach, in this case to research into perception, was at the heart of gestalt psychology. Arnheim acknowledged the enormity of the task for the child of representing what they see. In learning to represent in drawing what they perceive the child must grapple with the complex problems of turning three-dimensional into two-dimensional versions of things. As they struggle, they become dissatisfied with lower stages of differentiation in drawings and grope for more sophisticated versions. They also progressively master techniques and the use of media.

Arnheim's belief that images 'spoke' directly to those who were open to seeing them also resonated with the ethos and assumptions of modern art.

In modern art imagery had moved away from the long established figurative conventions of portraits, landscapes and still lives and become increasingly abstract. Colour, line, shape, texture and form were explored without the constraints of representation. Photography could now 'do' representation much better. In this climate, children's art and so-called primitive art were seen to exemplify admirably unspoiled, unschooled and free expression. For example Paul Klee wrote that 'The pictures of my little boy Felix are often better than mine because mine have often been filtered through the brain'(cited in Wilson 1992: 18). In the world of early childhood education this admiration for 'unspoiled' children's art crystallized into reification of 'the innocent eye' of children and the message that intervention by an adult in children's 'natural' creativity in drawing was inappropriate.

So in the course of a hundred years of art education the pendulum had swung from one extreme to another. At one extreme, in the elementary schools of the nineteenth century, drawing was perceived as one element in the instrumental preparation of children for citizenship and work. At the other extreme, in the nursery and infant schools of the twentieth century, drawing had come to be perceived as a somewhat romanticized 'natural unfolding' of individual children's talents. It was time for someone to reconcile these opposing views.

In the United States Eisner (1972), referred to in Chapter 1, challenged the ideology of development as a 'natural unfolding'. He recognized the importance of children learning from both experiences and instruction in art. He fore-grounded the communicative aspects of drawing and argued that learning 'moves from sensory perception to conception and then representation in forms that can be shared publicly'. (Elland 2002: 63) The sharing might be in talk, dramatic play or drawings. The role of the adult in art education was seen to be in ensuring that the child's experiences were rich in stimuli and in guiding them towards models of how they might develop ways of expressing themselves. Art educators of the period in the UK such as Gentle (1978), Morgan (1988) and Clement (1986) reflected this balanced approach.

In the UK Athey (1990) approached the study of children's drawings from a rather different perspective. She explored the idea of schemas, 'patterns of repeatable behaviour into which experiences are assimilated and that are gradually co-ordinated. Co-ordinations lead to higher-level and more powerful schemas' (Athey 1990: 37). Over a five-year period in the 1970s she studied the types of schemas – such as dynamic circular, enclosure, developing and containing space, dynamic vertical, rotation – produced by 2- to 5-year-old children in the Froebel Educational Institute nursery at Roehampton College and in the children's home settings. An important aspect of her work was that she liaised closely with the children's parents and nursery staff in generating her evidence. She argued that children were preoccupied at periods of their development by a schema type. Traces of their preoccupation were recorded in their drawings, language and play behaviours. For example a child might repeatedly draw circles, be fascinated by circular objects, enjoy running around in circles and respond to games (such as Ring a Roses) or narratives where circles figured. She identified three developmental stages related to schema: motor level, symbolic representation and thought level. There are obvious links between the Stage Theories of universal patterns of development, such as Kellogg's or Lowenfield's and Schema theories. Athey's work has been taken up by those working with under-5s, but there is scope for exploring more thoroughly the relationship between schemas and the development of symbol systems such as language, drawing and writing beyond the pre-school sector.

Matthews is both an artist and an art educator. His longitudinal studies using the 'naturalistically sensitive techniques' of observation, photography and videoing of his children (Matthews 1994), and latterly his grandchildren (1999), in their art making in home contexts have provided a richness of information about the behaviours of young children engaged in drawing and painting. He argues that all children's mark making is intentional: 'Far from being meaningless, the early paintings and drawings are products of a complex family of representational and expressive modes' (Matthews 1999: 21). He observes how the physical movements of very young children define three basic types of marks: vertical and horizontal arcs and push-pull action. His research is a rare example of considering the interweaving of the psycho-motor, aesthetic and cognitive aspects of drawing development. This is exemplified in Figure 2.1, a chart designed to illustrate his model of the development of drawing.

He writes about configurative and dynamic modes in children's representations which 'sweep through all aspects of representation like "waves" through different streams of intelligence. Configurative modes of action capture the shape and structure of objects; dynamic modes of representations record or monitor the movement of events or objects, often seen or imagined' (Matthews 1999: 155). An example of his painstaking observations is:

> Joel in my studio at fourteen months waves a paintbrush in horizontal arcs. He causes droplets to fly around in a beautiful arc, according to centrifugal or inertial forces; and when he stabs the brush against the empty air, in a vigorous up and downward overarm arc, inertial force causes droplets of paint to splatter onto the floor. In the first condition, a line of spots is made; in the second, a cluster of spots. In both situations he carefully visually tracks the effects he makes. He also visually monitors the large horizontal arc he makes on the floor, with a brush.
>
> (Matthews 1999: 23)

Children	
Birth – 1 year	• imitate actions and movement using their whole body
	• are aware of patterns which have strong contrasts and resemble the human face
	• make intentional marks, for example, with food using finger and hand
	• are aware that movements result in a mark
1–2 years	• make a variety of marks, sometimes described as scribbling
	• are aware that different movements make different marks
	• grip pen or crayon using palm of hand
	• make marks which record and represent the movement of their bodies and other objects
	• draw overlapping and layered marks
2–3 years	• use pincer grip to hold graphic materials
	• produce continuous line and closed shape to represent inside and outside
	• combine lines and shapes
	• produce separate but linked shapes
3–4 years	• name marks, and symbolic representation is emerging
	• experiment with the variety of marks that can be made by different graphic materials, tools and surfaces
	• unaided, use a circle plus lines to represent a person, often referred to as a 'tadpole person'
	• start to produce visual narratives
4–5 years	• are able to produce a range of shapes and sometimes combine them, for example, to produce a sun
	• draw shapes and figures that appear to float in space on the page
	• draw figures which include more details, such as arms, legs, hands, fingers, eyebrows
	• subdivide space on page to show higher and lower
At 6 years	• draw figures that are grounded and use lines for ground and the sky
	• display depth by making figures in the distance smaller to indicate further away
	• include more detail in their drawings, for example, windows, doors and chimneys on buildings
	• drawings have more narrative features, for example, may feature a number of episodes of the same story

Figure 2.1 The development of drawing (Matthews in Rodger 1999: 132)

Technical aspects of drawing development

In parallel to the study of broad aspects of drawing development gained from longitudinal or cross-sectional studies of children drawing and small scale case studies, some psychologists have carried out experimental, often laboratory-based, research into the detail of how children progress in technical aspects of drawing. The challenge has been to tease out whether young children are drawing what they *know* or what they *see* (Freeman 1980). The studies have focused on how children plan, sequence and make marks that are for them acceptable equivalencies of representing a three-dimensional world in two-dimensional lines. Much of the research is reported in journals specializing in cognitive psychology in language inaccessible to generalist readers. However, two researchers in the UK, Willatts and Cox, have made a point of writing up their work in styles and outlets accessible to educationalists.

Both researchers have set up experiments to study the way young children cope with the challenges of drawing objects set behind or within other objects (occlusion), different viewpoints of objects and places (spatial orientation and perspective) and representing human figures (Willatts 1977, 1995; Cox 1991, 1992). Their research has been driven by questions such as why young children have a tendency to draw objects as canonical representations drawing on their image of its key features: for example, why a table is often shown with four legs drawn from an 'aerial' view or a dog generally drawn from the side with four legs and a profile head. They have used laboratory-based experiments to explore how children cope with representing 'occlusion', that is objects such as fruit placed behind or inside other objects. They have investigated how children draw things from different points of view and how they learn the intricacies of depicting depth using the Western art conventions of perspective developed during the Renaissance. Both researchers are sensitive to the need to present experimental tasks to children embedded in their everyday realities or narratives familiar to children and to use appropriate language in dialogue with the children during experiments.

Cox has been particularly careful to apply her empirical research findings to the 'real world' of education. For example, she drew on a collection of children's drawings of human figures donated by a nursery headteacher to apply her research to teaching under-5s to draw (Cox 1997). She also applied her research to Key Stage One classrooms. She worked with an art educator and teacher to evaluate an approach to teaching drawing to 5- to 7-year-olds (Cooke *et al.* 1998). The approach, called 'negotiated drawing', incorporated careful observation and discussion of objects before drawing them. They were able to demonstrate that their approach to teaching drawing enhanced children's drawing capabilities.

A recent study (Whitbread and Leeder 2003) investigated how eighty

3- to 7-year-old children in UK primary classrooms solved the graphic problems of representing a man and a dog. Whitbread and Leeder were interested in the development of levels of differentiation of the distinctive features of the man and dog in the children's drawings. As one might expect, the degree and sophistication of differentiation increased with age/maturity. More contentiously they investigated the sequences in which children made marks to represent the figures. On the basis of their evidence, they hypothesize that the graphical sequence in which the children tackled the challenges of representing the man and dog had an effect on the quality of the drawing. They suggest that adults might introduce children to the range of sequences available to them in drawing figures in order to model approaches to 'better' drawings of figures. This recommendation raises interesting pedagogic issues about 'teaching' young children to draw and about how much adult intervention is appropriate.

Another important source of experimental research has been the field of art therapy where children's drawings are used as windows on their emotional states. The work is best exemplified by Malchiodi (1998) who combines her clinical experience with a grasp of research in the field. She argues for the importance of acknowledging the multi-dimensional aspects of children's drawings: a combination of the child's stage of development, individual experiences and feelings and the socio-cultural influences and contexts in which they draw or paint. There has also been interest in research into children with unusual drawing abilities: for example, the study of Nadia, an autistic child (Selfe 1977).

Finally, in the study of 'technical' aspects of children's drawings, there has been research into the manifestations of cultural differences in pedagogy, life styles and imagery in young children's artwork. For example, Cox (1993) discusses the cultural influences of Australian Aboriginal imagery on children's drawings collected for a BBC/Open University television programme on children's drawings. Aboriginal children were fluent in drawing in the Warlpiri and the Western styles of depiction, or using a combination, in their artwork. Cox (1997) and Wilson (1985) also studied the artwork of young children educated in the very different traditions of China. Wilson studied young children's drawings in Holland (Wilson and Ligtvoet 1992) and Matthews (1997) in Singapore.

The influence of socio-cultural contexts on children's drawing

So what does all this research tell us about *why children draw*? We can see that the explanations incorporate a complex mixture of the nature and nurture debate. From the perspective of 'natural' development, it is clear that children use drawings as a tool for understanding and representing important aspects of their own personal, lived experiences of people, places and things. Beyond coming to terms with personal experiences, their representations serve the function of exploring 'big ideas' common to all our lives, like dependence and dominance, good and evil, danger and adventure. The power of visual narratives in communities for confronting these kinds of abstractions has been potent throughout history. Visual narratives exploring 'big ideas' have ranged from those produced in charcoal and soot on walls in cave art to the electronic, digital media of video art.

Reasons reflecting the nurture aspects of the debate are embedded in the cultural conventions of graphical representations surrounding young children in their habitats. Children learn to imitate existing models of drawing in comics, advertisements, cartoons and computer games. Yet, as with 'popular' versions of literacy modelled in magazines, advertisement jingles, pop songs and toys, schools treat such influences with suspicion. In educational contexts there is a strong urge to maintain a construct of the young child as 'innocent', and popular, media driven graphics have long been seen as somehow corrupting to very young minds (Wilson and Wilson 1977).

Our second question at the beginning of the chapter was, *why children do not draw?* It is well documented that children's early drawings are characterized by a 'creativity' which somehow becomes stultified into 'the conventionalised drawings of middle childhood' (Davis and Gardner 1992: 192). If children are not encouraged to persevere in learning to draw, within school or home contexts, they are likely to remain arrested in the drawing capabilities of an 8-year-old. Many adults are self-conscious about their inadequacy in drawing and shrink from doing so in public.

In the next chapter we will be introduced to a project which attempted to track the progress of a small group of young children over a three-year period in home and school contexts as they learned to draw and to assume identities as creators of drawings. We will explore what motivated them to draw and what discouraged them. We will look at their personal journeys towards graphicacy as well as the impact of the social contexts in which they made those journeys.

3   Overview of the project

Aims of the project

Our aim in the project was to try to find out what influenced a group of young children's drawing behaviours in the contrasting contexts of home and school. We were interested in how, as the contexts changed (for example as their domestic lives altered or as they moved from pre-school to Key Stage One classrooms) their drawings reflected these changes. We were also interested in how the beliefs about drawing of significant adults in the children's lives affected how they drew and what they drew. Because we were collecting evidence over a three-year period, we were able to observe changes in how the children were learning to draw and how drawing was helping them to learn in formal and informal settings.

We selected a group of four boys and three girls from a range of socio-economic backgrounds and geographical areas. Figure 3.1 summarizes the characteristics of the seven children we tracked over the period of the project. We will be finding out more about their individual stories later in the book.

It is important also to understand the impact of the contexts in which we observed the children over the three years. For example, it was quite shocking for us to realize how fragmented their experiences of early childhood education were. We chose to observe them each year for a month in the early autumn, partly because we knew that during these months the children were likely to be involved in transitions to new phases of their lives at school. Continuities and discontinuities are always thrown into sharpest relief at points of transition. We did not anticipate the scale of the discontinuities these young children were to experience. All seven children had moved physically to different buildings or to different spaces within a building and had new key workers each year we went back to work with them. This level of dislocation of young children in their early experiences of pre-school and first years at school would be unthinkable in other cultural contexts. For example in Scandinavian and other European systems the expectation is that children remain with the same key worker throughout their kindergarten experience, often until they are 6.

Of course the children were also experiencing changes in their domestic lives – new babies, different homes and reconfigurations in their immediate

Child	Age	Siblings	Occupation of mother	Occupation of father	Setting attended	Location of setting
Luke	3 yrs 0 mths	One younger brother	Part-time supermarket checkout operator	Long distance lorry driver	Day-care setting (called a Family Centre)	Inner city area characterized by high levels of poverty, unemployment and poor quality council housing.
Donna	3 yrs 8 mths	Only child	Full-time mother (previously bar worker)	Scaffolder		
Jake	4 yrs 0 mths	One older sister	Part-time literacy support teacher	Refractory engineer	Nursery class of infant school	Long-established school on the outskirts of a city but classed as 'inner city'. Housing predominantly private with large older properties being converted by young families. Many established local families. Community made up of a mixture of professionals, skilled workers and those working in service industries. Children of ethnic minority: 25%.
Simon	4 yrs 1 mth	One older sister	Full-time mother (previously radiographer)	Salesman (industry)		
Holly	4 yrs 6 mths	One younger brother and one younger sister	Full-time mother (previously nursery assistant and nanny)	Process operator in chemical industry		
Edward	4 yrs 9 mths	One older sister	Checkout operator	Engineer	Parallel reception classes of primary school	Inner suburbs of large city. Newly built school in a mixed private and council house area. Community made up of mainly young families with parents in skilled work or service industries.
Lianne	5 yrs 0 mths	One older brother	Classroom assistant in school attended by Lianne	Skilled technical worker		

Figure 3.1 Characteristics of seven children

and extended family structures – to which they were having to adapt. Outside school, families were going through similar changes in roles and responsibilities, fluctuations in partnerships, employment, home ownership and parenting that characterize the complexity of all family lives today.

Research methods

In the first year of the project we approached parents via the managers of the pre-school settings which the children were attending. We selected pairs of children who were attending a range of types of pre-school provision. The parents and practitioners responsible for the children were asked if they would like to be involved in the project. The families lived in different geographical areas and were representative of a range of socio-economic backgrounds. Because of the small-scale nature of the project we did not include the additional complexity of children whose first language was not English. There have been some fascinating studies of bilingual children and early literacy (for example see the edited collection by Gregory 1997) but little on early drawing of children in dual language households at the start of school. This is an area ripe for research.

We used two main methods to collect evidence about the seven children's drawings. First, each year of the project we gave the parents and key workers a large scrapbook and an easy to use disposable camera with a flash facility. We asked them to collect any paintings or drawings the children did over the period of a month at home or school. Then they were asked to stick them in the scrapbook and to make notes for us about the times and contexts in which the children drew and the purposes of the activities. We were interested in looking for relationships between the children's two-dimensional and three-dimensional meaning making and representations. We also asked them to take photographs of the children involved in play activities using small figures, blocks or objects around the house and in role-play. We asked the parents and practitioners to annotate them, as they had the artwork, and add them to the scrapbooks. Examples of the scrap book entries, one from home and one from school, are in Figures 3.2 and 3.3. Each year, we photocopied the scrapbooks and photos full size and in colour for the parents and practitioners and gave them the copies as a thank you for working with us.

Second, each year we interviewed the parents – usually the mother but sometimes the mother with the father – and the key worker or teacher both before we asked them to collect the drawings and after they had done so. We used the scrapbooks as a stimulus for a dialogue with the parents and practitioners, and later with the children, about the children's meaning making. All of the interviews were tape recorded and transcribed. We made fieldnotes and took digital photographs in each setting to capture contextual

Everyone is coming to see the King and the Queen. we couldn't find the queen so we just used the dog. The wall is for the traffic so the people have to stay in the castle because the wall is there.

This took place at teatime, (5:30pm) Just before this the children were putting the toys away but got distracted.

Holly's brother Andy was with her and they did this together. Andy didn't really make any comments

After this Holly had her dessert. She had already eaten her tea.

Figure 3.2 Example from home scrapbook

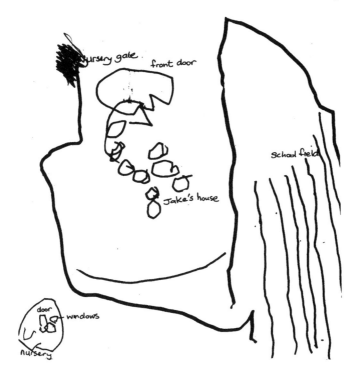

Figure 3.3 Example from school scrapbook.

1.45 p.m. 15 mins. Key adult introduced new artefacts into wet sand area to stimulate children into devising an imaginary route from home to nursery e.g. buildings made by children – houses, shops, figures (lollipop lady, children) petrol station, cars, etc. Jake worked in sand further 20 mins after input. Left area and joined his friend drawing a plan of his journey from home to nursery (stimulated by key adult). Jake decided independently to draw his own plan. Eager to discuss his work with both peers and key adult on completion – 10 mins.

information about both the home and the school contexts in which the children had produced their drawings. We invited groups of the practitioners from the project to meet and help us to make sense of the seven sets of scrapbooks and notes. We were searching for patterns and themes emerging across the evidence from the sample of seven children, as well as themes emerging from studying the individual cases.

We experimented with approaches to accessing the children's perspectives on their drawings. As other researchers have discovered (for example Grieg and Taylor 1999; Lewis and Lindsay 2000; Clark and Moss 2001), gaining access to young children's beliefs is challenging both methodologically and ethically. When we tried talking with them the tendency for us to slip into 'teacher questions and child responds' was hard to escape, particularly within school settings. Drummond (1998) describes this feature of adult/child interactions in early childhood settings as benevolent but relentless questioning. The greater the gap between the children's drawing and the attempts to get the children to discuss the drawings with us, the less fruitful these discussions were.

A more productive strategy to get a conversation rather than a question and answer routine established was for the researcher to withdraw completely from the dialogue about drawings. The child was invited to choose a friend to show and talk about their scrapbooks, whilst the researcher sat quietly and made notes on the peer group conversations. But we found that the most effective strategy to gain access to the children's views was to get the children to respond playfully to a chart showing aspects of 'play' and 'work' activities including two-dimensional and three-dimensional artwork (See Figure 3.4). They were asked to draw faces which reflected how they felt about a range of activities in which they were involved at home and school, including drawing, and to talk to the researcher about what those activities involved.

Ethical considerations

Of course this approach to 'listening to children's voices' involved us in ethical considerations. There has been growing concern about the rights of young children involved in research projects. For example Alderson (1995) argues that the Convention on the Rights of Children (United Nations 1989) and the Children Act (Department of Health 1989) provide frameworks for not only the protection of children but for respectful ways of researching with rather than on them. However, there are pressures both politically and domestically to treat children as 'powerless'. Choices are made about children's approaches to citizenship, preparation for work and even their approach to religious education within our school systems. Parents are often consumed by media and family expectations to groom their children for 'success'. The dominance of adults in children's decisions about most aspects of their educational and domestic lives is still paramount. It is challenging to find ways of redressing adult dominance in research with young children.

For example, adult dominance is reflected in the approach we took to gaining 'informed consent' from participants in our project. It was the parents of the children who gave us this written informed consent. Although researchers have claimed that children under the age of 5 understand the principles and can respond to informed consent procedures (and in fact we have heard one conference paper presentation making such claims for 3-year-olds), it is difficult to believe that they can understand the consequences of such consent. It is fair to say that many adults who sign informed consent forms do not fully understand the consequences of participating in research projects.

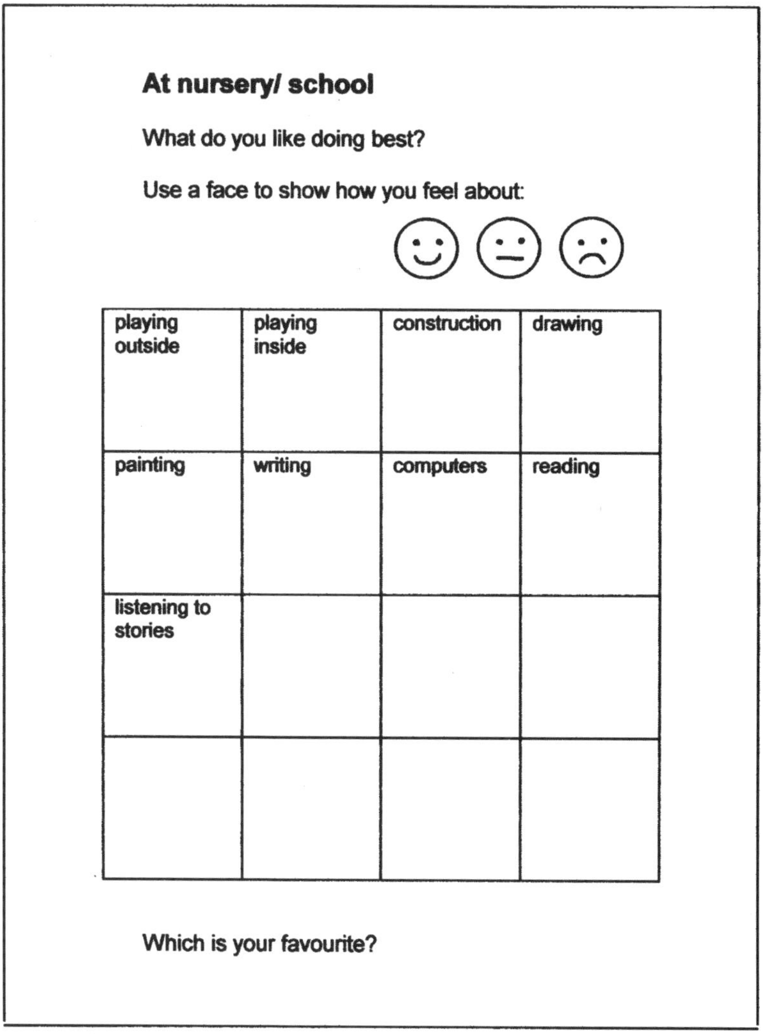

At nursery/ school

What do you like doing best?

Use a face to show how you feel about:

playing outside	playing inside	construction	drawing
painting	writing	computers	reading
listening to stories			

Which is your favourite?

Figure 3.4 Page taken from 'smiley face' questionnaire

What we were able to do was to ensure that throughout the three years our approaches to research with the children were:

- respectful (in that we always made it clear that they could withdraw at any time);
- sensitive (in that we tried to ensure that they were given some autonomy in the processes of sharing ideas with us);

- age appropriate (in that methods were geared to their developmental levels and involved them in motivating, fun activities with us);
- caring (in that the researcher developed an emotional rapport with the children and their families over the three-year period);
- ensuring confidentiality (through anonymizing the contexts and people involved, and asking for consent for images to be released for dissemination and publication of the project findings).

Kathy, as the researcher and co-author, also worked hard at the ethical aspects of researching with the parents of the children. She made sure that the practitioners selected only families to approach who were confident enough in their parenting to work with us. She explained clearly to them – both by letter and when she visited them at home – exactly what their involvement in the project would mean in terms of time, activities and responsibilities. She was careful to be respectful and sensitive to the family's cultures and domestic lives. They were allowing us to enter their domestic worlds. She negotiated times for home visits around their needs. This often meant going to the homes in the evenings. If this were the case she kept in touch by mobile phone to ensure her own personal safety. She attuned herself to each family situation, 'reading' their emotional state and current preoccupations from their verbal and non-verbal behaviours. As an experienced early childhood educator, she often found herself engaging in conversations with the parents about broad aspects of the children's development and education. But she was careful not to comment directly on aspects of the children's current schooling about which she had information and, indeed, views. The fact that none of the families or schools withdrew from the project during the three-year study is probably the best testament to her sensitivity as a researcher.

We had to be equally sensitive to being respectful of the practitioners involved in the project. Our initial contacts were with the managers of settings, and through them we approached, initially, pre-school practitioners working with the children. However, as the children made transitions each autumn to new settings or classrooms, each year Kathy had to gain access to different sets of teachers or key workers. Again we applied the principles of respect, acknowledging their pressurized working lives and personal autonomy in working with them. We tried to ensure that they benefited from cooperation with the project by involving them in follow-up meetings, sharing home insights into the children's passions and preoccupations and gifting them a copy of the children's scrap books.

Getting practitioners and parents to say what they know

We found that using visual images – the children's work and photographs – was productive in getting both parents and practitioners to talk about what they believed. As we have already argued, reading visual images is an everyday skill. Yet research using visual imagery as prompts or evidence in research is in the early stages of development. As Prosser (1998: 100) argues, qualitative research 'uses words or occasionally numbers and only very rarely images except as representation of words and numbers'. We were anxious to use a participatory approach to research. This approach is being developed in particular in evaluations at local levels of services for families such as those being developed in Sure Start programmes (see Brodie 2003). We found that the visual evidence was useful to us in getting the parents, practitioners and children into conversations which had an enjoyable and clear focus to them. Most people enjoy looking at and commenting on photographs and pictures rather than being asked to respond to interview questions about quite abstract ideas.

Photographs also captured invaluable, contextual evidence for us. A picture tells a thousand words. The images we captured of the educational settings attended by the children over the three years told us much about the belief systems of the adults who had organized the spaces, sited the furniture and placed the objects there. For example, Figures 3.5 to 3.8 show the features of settings from Nursery, Reception, Year One and Year Two. It is quite clear in analysing even cursorily the images that the equipment, furniture, objects and displays on the walls reflect the inevitable shift from practical, play-based activities at the Foundation Stage to seat-based, disembedded activities focused on literacy and numeracy at Key Stage One.

Analysing the evidence

The great challenge of qualitative research is to find ways of analysing the evidence you collect that are manageable. Many qualitative researchers collect far too much data without having thought through how to make sense of it. It is important to plan ahead to how you will tackle the task of analysis before you are faced with box files bulging with data. A theoretical framework should also inform your analysis. Yet within this predetermined framework you need the flexibility to test out hunches and ideas against evidence at each stage of the analysis. This is the mechanism by which you develop themes.

We took the children's activities as the starting point for the analysis. In analysing the children's drawings we were not interested in developmental criteria (such as those of Kellogg or Matthews described in Chapter 2) or

Figure 3.5 Nursery setting

Figure 3.6 Reception setting

Figure 3.7 Year One setting

Figure 3.8 Year Two setting

technical criteria (such as those used by Willatts and Cox also referenced in Chapter 2). Our lens was a socio-cultural one. Our focus was on the influences of the historical, social and cultural features of the environments on what and how children drew.

Initially we concentrated on the content and style of the drawings. We coded the content of the drawings under the broad headings of people, places and things and quality of interaction. We looked for similarities and differences in the contexts in which the children had produced their drawings using fieldnotes and photographs as our evidence base. We used the interview data to access the beliefs of the significant adults – parents and practitioners – about the role of drawing in these seven young children's meaning making. We also noted where the children's passions and preoccupations (media, hobbies, family and friendship relationships) and personal styles were represented in their drawings.

As the project developed, we moved backwards and forwards between socio-cultural theoretical perspectives and our accumulated evidence. We tried to map out the individual pathways of the children towards graphicacy against the contextual features of their journeys. After some false starts and many hours of debate, the domains we chose to manage and analyse the data were:

- observed and recorded child behaviours;
- distinctive features of the environment;
- values and beliefs of significant adults;
- adult styles of interaction;
- adult views of the children's behaviours;
- children's views of their own behaviours.

Of course the exciting bit about research is what you find out. And that is what we will turn to in the next few chapters. But it is important when reading about research findings to understand and critique the methods by which they have been reached. We hope this chapter has given you sufficient insight into our research methods to be able to do so.

4 Luke's story

In the next four chapters we will follow the stories of four of the seven children, two boys and two girls, to illustrate some of the ideas explored in the opening two chapters on young children's meaning making and drawing at home and school. We will be reporting the voices of the parents, practitioners and children as they talked with us about the children and their drawings.

Luke at home aged 3

At the start of the project Luke (at just 3) was the youngest child we followed. He lived in an inner city council house. He attended a Family Centre three days a week along with his younger brother. His mother was the dominant adult at home, as his father, a long distance driver, was absent during the week. Even at weekends Luke's father had little involvement in playing with his sons. Saturday was the family shopping day. On Sundays, while their mother worked a shift at a local supermarket, the young brothers were taken to their paternal grandparents.

Luke's life was controlled by daily and weekly patterns of events. He liked routines and became upset if they were disrupted. At home he was concerned that everything was kept in its place. Luke's mother saw this meticulous approach to his environment as a characteristic of the child. However, she herself organized the space within the home well and had socialized the children into playing their part. The two boys learned, for example, where their dirty clothes had to be put – not thrown on the bedroom floor! There was an expectation that they would put their toys away at the end of an afternoon of free play.

Luke's mother modelled and supported particular forms of meaning making. Children's television and videos were a big part of the day. She enjoyed watching them as much as the children did. She often referred to favourite media characters in conversations around the house and built references to them into their joint play episodes. As reported in Marsh's (2002) study of 3-year-olds, everyday exchanges about television and video characters took part within joint involvement episodes on the floor in front of the television. Luke's drawing, 'Strawberry eating a little boy from the Fruit

Pastille advert' (Figure 4.1), was his response to a television advertisement for Fruit Pastilles featuring a huge strawberry devouring a small boy. His mother told us: 'When he watches you can see him backing away from the telly'.

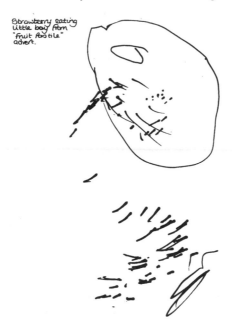

Strawberry eating little boy from "fruit Pastille" advert.

Figure 4.1 Strawberry eating little boy from the Fruit Pastille advert

Luke's mother included an element of scariness within her playful interactions with the boys. They had a 'silly time' when they sang and danced together at the end of the day. The drawings Luke completed at home during this period revealed a fertile imagination and a preoccupation with 'scary' things. He drew a crocodile with sharp teeth and scary legs. His mother told us that they sang together the song she had learned at Pontins as a child, Never Smile at a Crocodile. Luke's fascination with crocodiles emerged in a narrative he wove into a play episode. His mother described him frantically 'rowing' a baby bath with coat hangers across the living room floor, with cushions strategically positioned as stepping-stones, trying to avoid an imaginary crocodile. With great speed the same coat hangers were transformed from fishing rods to oars as Luke's imaginative play script developed. Figure 4.2 is the drawing he made to re-represent this exciting game. It was one of many examples we had of boys' 'action drawings'.

Luke was only allowed to use a 'megasketcher' for drawing in the lounge. He used it for the recording and erasing of continuous rotations, drawn

Figure 4.2 Action drawing

quickly and with great energy. These were Luke's private drawings, requiring no input or feedback from his mother. Paper, pens and scissors were reserved for use at the kitchen table when his younger brother was taking his afternoon nap. Luke's fascination with scissors began with his mother cutting out butterflies for him to colour. She recollected her own love of cutting out as a child. Luke's current preoccupation was with systematically cutting paper into strips, turning each strip at a right angle and cutting it into a smaller strip until he was left with tiny pieces of paper. Sometimes he made a mark on the paper as a prop for his cutting action. Whilst cutting or drawing at the kitchen table as his mother pottered around doing chores, Luke involved her in listening to his monologue. She recognized that, like her, Luke was a great talker. In his monologues, he wove stories around his cut outs, stimulated by their shapes. He would pause occasionally to check she was listening. She told us, 'He'll cut out something not trying to make the shape, then he'll see it fall down and he'll say, "Oh look, I've made a triangle!" He'll pretend he made it properly'.

When mother and son drew together at the kitchen table there was an interesting reciprocity to their interactions, quite unlike those he would have in the Family Centre around drawing episodes. His meticulous way of working made him critical of his mother's attempts to draw television characters accurately. For example, she had struggled to draw the Teletubbies for him and reported the dialogue between mother and son: 'I did La La and he said, "La La's head doesn't go like that". You've got to have the right colour, the right shade'. Luke clearly felt an equal partner in these dialogues.

Luke aged 3 at the Family Centre

The routine at the Family Centre was for the morning to be spent in 'free flow', with free choice of activities and spaces allocated to a particular type of activity such as large construction play. For the afternoon sessions the children were allocated to a base under the supervision of their key worker. At 3 years old Luke was a tentative, nervous participant in Family Centre activities. He appeared to be reliant on his key worker. She commented on his ability to enter into long monologues about home events with adults, using what she described as 'the language of a much older child' with many 'adult phrases'. During the morning free flow activities he watched the activity of older boys warily. He would venture out into the centre play areas to find his key worker with the reassurance of a book firmly clutched under one arm. If his key adult was not available he would search for his substitute comfort figure, 4-year-old Rebecca, who would respond by firmly taking hold of his hand.

Within the Family Centre Luke attempted to re-create the joint involvement episodes he enjoyed with his mother at the kitchen table. For example, he involved his key worker in a recurring play script of a 'tea party' to hold her attention. Luke also used the tea party script to satisfy his preoccupation with cutting materials into strips as he cut clay or dough into 'food'. His preferred activities were cutting paper, modelling with dough and watching videos – all activities familiar to him at home. He demonstrated an unusual ability to become totally absorbed in video and television imagery, in what Csiksentmihalyi (1979) called a 'flow' state. Each afternoon his key worker tried to interest him in the set craft activity, usually involving paint or glue. Luke was a reluctant participant. The boys were kept immaculately clean in the home setting by their mum. Luke was unhappy when his hands got glue or paint on them.

In 1996, at the start of our project, Desirable Outcomes for Children's Learning on Entering Compulsory Education (DfEE/SCAA 1996), were introduced into all settings offering an educational component to their services for 3- and 4-year-olds. Family Centre practitioners felt under pressure to channel children towards 'educational' outcomes from activities in the centre. This included shaping children's mark making towards emergent writing and recognizable drawings. Drawing was now interpreted as a stage towards children becoming literate and included in the child's developmental record as progression from horizontal and vertical marks through figure drawing and on to early writing. This checklist of competencies, shared with parents at progress meetings, seemed to dominate the key workers' agenda. It influenced their approach to drawing activities, dominated their discussions with children about the content of their drawings and preoccupied them in completing the children's records. The centre staff considered that Luke's mother

Figure 4.3 Mammy

was pushing him to write before he was ready. Using the checklist for the Family Centre records as a tool for persuasion, they told her that it was important that he did not miss out on drawing figures before he started to write. At the centre they concentrated on Luke's ability to draw figures.

Figure 4.3, Mammy, was drawn following the key worker's modelling of how to draw a human figure. Luke was encouraged to draw a circle and shown where to put the eyes and nose. His only decision was to draw the hair. Luke's key workers admitted that they were unsure of how to interact with a child who was drawing. There was a presumption that every child should be able to draw the key people in their lives, particularly mummy. They acknowledged that some children had difficulty in drawing people but felt that it was acceptable to coach a child as long as they were 'ready'. Luke worked hard to ensure his representation of his mum closely resembled his key worker's model. This didactic approach to drawing did little to encourage and value the kind of spontaneous and exuberant meaning making Luke was choosing to do at home. It had little in common with Matthews (1999) or Malchiodi's (1998) beliefs about the role of drawing in supporting the child's developing sense of self. As a result Luke rarely chose to draw in the Family Centre context.

Luke aged 4 at home

A year later we went back to visit Luke in the new family home in a quiet cul-de-sac. Luke's preferred pattern of drawing at the kitchen table and chatting with his mother as she was occupied with household tasks had been interrupted. His younger brother no longer had an afternoon nap and drawing was limited to when Mum could sit with both children and supervise them. This put her under pressure and she sometimes had to defer to their requests to do some drawings. 'They sometimes see it [on the shelf] and say, "Can we draw?" or "Can we paint?" and I'll say "Not now" or "Maybe later". Paint at nursery. Out of sight out of mind.'

When they did all sit together at the kitchen table, the 'educational agenda' of the Family Centre was still impacting on Luke's mother's approach to drawing. She was frustrated by attempts to persuade him to draw representations of figures. She asked him to copy pictures. 'When you see a picture, and you say to him, "Can you draw a picture of a whatever?" he'll try to draw it. But because it doesn't look exactly like a pig, he'll say it's rubbish, and if it is the megasketcher the zipper goes down and he won't even have it on.' Luke, in turn frustrated by what he saw to be his inability to draw things that looked 'right', made scornful comments about his mother's and younger brother's drawings. 'That doesn't look nowt like a house. That doesn't look nowt like a cat. Where's its tail?' The drawings collected by Luke's mother during the second year of the project reflected her attempts to support his drawing and were probably mostly instigated by her. The drawing of his brother, given to him as a birthday card (Figure 4.4) was the only evidence of Luke drawing freely on paper. This was still, however, probably completed at his mother's request and in her presence.

Luke's mother had been advised by staff from the Family Centre to provide materials to support Luke in learning to write. With practice Luke could now recognize and write his name. His mother was proud of this but admitted that writing, and trying to get him to write numbers, was stressful for Luke. She commented that he got really anxious and upset that he could not do it right. However, she had bought some worksheets for Luke to do at home which provided more enjoyable times together: 'We've got this learning to write thing and its like mazes when you've got to go a certain way, and he's fantastic with them. He loves doing them, going through the gaps and doing squiggles'.

In contrast to Luke's frustration with drawing and writing, Luke's mother and key worker reported his increasing use of role-play to act out both real life experiences and re-enact video scripts. In representing real life experiences, his mother described his preoccupation with using a tape measure around the house – 'As soon as he sees it [the tape measure] it's gone, it's disappeared, it's clipped onto his trousers and he's a workman'. Following a traumatic visit

Figure 4.4 Birthday card

with his asthmatic brother to hospital, Luke played out the role of the doctor. He also assumed the role of his key worker, both at home and at the Family Centre, turning a book around when reading it to show the pictures to other (real or imagined) children. At the Family Centre his favourite book was *Funny Bones* (Ahlberg and Ahlberg 1993) reflecting his persistent love/hate relationship with frightening images.

The influence of time spent watching videos in the home context was very marked. His mother discussed how he used familiar objects available in his immediate environment to support him in playing out a role, having memorized the script of the key player. It was obvious that Luke's mother gained pleasure from her son's interest in popular cultural artefacts, reflecting Marsh's (2001) findings of parents' active acceptance of the pervasive nature of media texts in the home. 'When it's on he just sits and watches it but afterwards he will do like pretending that he is in that film or is that character. Nine times out of ten he's the baddy.' When watching a video Luke also found the toys bought from the Disney Shop associated with it. His mother reported one such episode: 'He had the radio cassette and the microphone on his lap, a little karaoke thing, and that's what he does, his character, Woody, in the film. Because they are all moving house and he is in charge and he's telling them to get a moving buddy, a partner, so that they won't get lost, and Luke is sat there copying it word for word' (Figure 4.5). Given the recent family history of moving house, this game was of particular intensity for Luke.

Figure 4.5 Media related play

The new house had a large garden into which children of a range of ages were invited to play. This ensured that under Luke's leadership complex play scripts could be re-enacted. His mother commented that broadening his circle of friendships had caused Luke to ask questions in his search for new meaning and understanding. She gave the following examples: 'Where do you go if you die? What if you are good? What if you are bad? He thinks that you have to be old and have a twisted neck before you die. When Hannah said her brother was in the graveyard: "What's he doing in there then?" "He died." "Children don't die." And they are arguing about it.'

Luke aged 4 in the Family Centre

Unlike practitioners in school settings, staff in the Family Centre did acknowledge the influence of media imagery on children's play. They knew about children's programmes, video games and passions. Now the oldest child in the nursery as others had left the centre to start school, Luke had grown in confidence and become a leader. This was manifested particularly in role-play. He used construction to support his dramatic play and often 'set up' the play scenario and invited other children to join him. He had strong ideas about how a particular 'story' should be re-enacted and complained to his mother when other children did not play 'properly' games such as 'Jurassic Park'.

'You just can't get them to do what you want … they want to go and play Mums and Dads'. His key worker reported: 'Some children will come over and stay for a little bit, but then if they don't do what he wants them to do, he says they are messing it up'. A recurring play theme of escaping from frightening situations characterized his play across both pre-school and home contexts. This ability to play out preoccupations that have a strong emotional content reflects the play literature (e.g. Sutton-Smith 1979; Paley 1986b). As a 4-year-old at the Family Centre he spent a short period of time each day with a small group of children doing seat-based 'school readiness' activities: learning to write their letters and numbers, to sit still while listening to stories and singing together. The children were expected to 'fit in' with what the adults instructed them to do and to 'sit down and respond when spoken to'.

Luke aged 5 at home

By the age of 5 Luke was drawing and writing a lot at home. Cupboards had recently been built in the dining room at home for storage of the children's toys, games and paper. Luke's mother felt this had influenced their choice of activities. The scissors and the Megasketcher were no longer readily available. Although the boys were able to get their own paper from the shelf, pens were kept in the mother's bedside cabinet. This control over key artefacts, enabled her to act as gatekeeper to their drawing activities. In fact Luke told us that he was not allowed to cut out any more at home. It seemed that Luke's mother felt that his preoccupation with scissors was not helping him to master the use of a pencil. But Luke seemed happy to draw. Despite these constraints, Luke had developed a new ability, partly the result of practice but also of physical maturing, to represent images in a way that he found satisfying. Now he was using drawings and symbols to communicate with others.

For example he used drawing as a way of capturing the stages of a story. 'Lots of little pictures' (Figure 4.6) was completed towards the end of his time at the Family Centre. Each small image was a separate story, which he told as he drew. The images represented experiences which had affected Luke emotionally: for example 'a machine sticking a needle into a baby' and 'me crying'. There were also images of recently 'discovered' animals and machinery which interested him. A wonderful 'Holiday diary' (Figure 4.7), completed by Luke and his mother together recorded the salient features of the family holiday experiences. It demonstrates how his mother helped him to combine the modes of drawing, writing and story and continued to be a 'drawing partner for her son'.

At age 5, Luke seemed to have made a huge leap in his physical development. He was much more physically daring. He displayed a range of new accomplishments, including climbing trees and jumping down stairs.

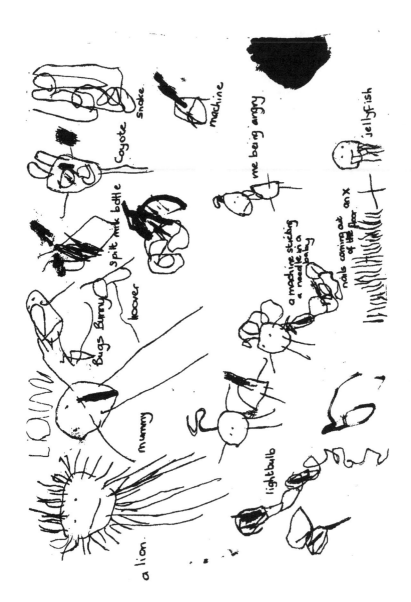

Figure 4.6 Lots of little pictures

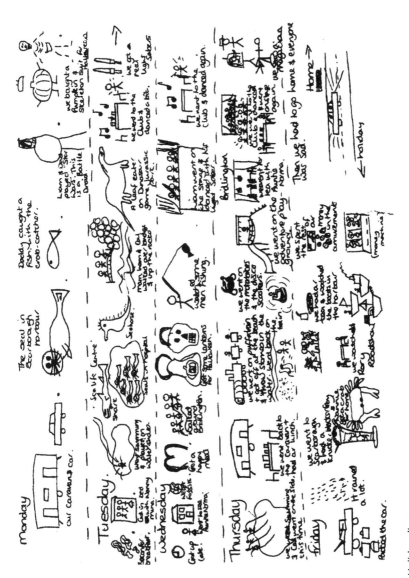

Figure 4.7 Holiday diary

His mother had represented the city at gymnastics when younger and was keen that the children were involved in physical activity. Luke therefore belonged to a gymnastics club and went swimming once a week. Other new skills included using bubble gum to blow bubbles, whistling, clicking his fingers and tying his shoelaces.

Towards the end of his time at the Family Centre staff thought that he was becoming over-confident and dominating younger children. His mother certainly thought he had changed. 'He's harder. He's not as sensitive and he's more rough.' She acknowledged the growing influence of Luke's father. He played a much stronger part in the upbringing of his two children now they were classed as 'boys' and no longer as 'babies'. Father and his young sons watched the television coverage of wrestling matches together. The play fighting between the boys and their dad following the programmes was encouraged by Luke's father as a way of 'toughening them up' in preparation for the world of school.

Luke aged 5 at school

When he transferred into the reception class of a Roman Catholic primary school at 5, a confident and experienced early years teacher taught Luke. In addition to her initial teacher training, she had completed an intensive early years course at the local university. This course had involved her in both theory and practice in relation to working with children of nursery age and informed her beliefs about the holistic needs of the children she taught. She was concerned to introduce formal education gradually, seeking to provide a balance of child and adult initiated activities in the reception class.

The children were allowed to draw whatever they wanted if a drawing table was set up, but the teacher commented that the children often replicated standard images and cited as an example a recent preponderance of drawing houses. The teacher was conscious of gender issues in relation to children's choices of activities. For example she told us that she had removed cars from the construction play area because it had led to the area being dominated by the boys. She felt that girls generally seemed to be more interested in drawing than boys. Yet she noted that Luke was often to be found in areas where he could draw. 'If he's in the office you could lose him virtually for the whole day.'

In this reception classroom Luke was lucky enough to have time and freedom to explore his preoccupations through drawing without adult direction. He had always been able to become immersed for long periods in activities that were meaningful to him. He was now motivated to draw because of a real sense of achievement. So when he showed us his drawing of a 'Machine for making bread' (Figure 4.8) he said with confidence, 'You'll love this'.

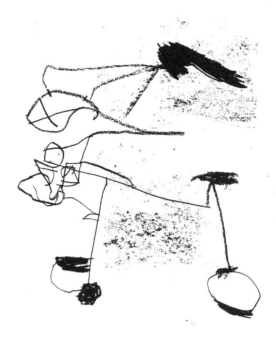

Figure 4.8   Machine for making bread

He had made a similar drawing the night before at home, which his mother had labelled as 'Bread making machine' (Figure 4.9). Perhaps he was trying to work through a number of connections in these drawings. The story of the Little Red Hen had been 'acted out' at school. He had experience of his nan's bread making machine. Finally he was developing a friendship with a boy who drew machines. Perhaps a combination of these interests led Luke to try to make sense through his drawings of the way a machine can deliver a loaf of bread.

The class teacher had noticed the children's need to chat about their drawings as they worked. She planned for a work experience girl to sit with the children at the drawing table. Her guidance to the teenager emphasized that she was not to draw for them but that she could point out inaccuracies if they were drawing, for example, a person. The class teacher commented that the young girl often just coloured in alongside the children. She reported that the teenager was 'quite arty and likes just sitting doodling'. Having an older girl modelling drawing behaviour at the table was attractive to Luke. It gave drawing status but also fulfilled his need to talk to an older child or an adult in a context in which power was evenly shared between him and a drawing partner. It re-enacted his drawing partnership with his mother.

At the age of 5 Luke seemed to be using drawing to explore and make connections across a broad range of interests. However, there was little

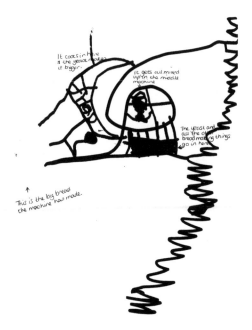

Figure 4.9 Bread making machine

evidence of the influence of cartoons, which had replaced his fascination with video images and stories, in his drawings in classroom-based 'educational' activities. He had learned that such imagery was not part of 'school' culture. It was only at playtime, surrounded by the same age or older boys, that Luke took part in animated discussions about video and cartoon characters. Playtime was when chasing and pretend fighting games flourished and his love/ hate relationship with scary images was nourished. This is illustrated in an intense discussion we recorded Luke having with a school friend.

> Luke: But you know what? One day, one night, my Dad told me this story and do you know what he said? This little boy went on holiday with his Uncle Nick and do you know what? One day the little boy looked out of the window at the field and they were playing football and he went to tell his Granddad and he said those are ghosts. And then the next night he stayed up really late and looked out of the window again and they were playing football again and guess what they were playing with? A head! Somebody's head!
>
> Scott: I've seen it real, me. I've seen someone kicking someone, a dead people.
>
> Luke: Oh, don't tell me about it, will you. Oh please don't. I'm not going to listen.

Scott: It's not scary; it's not scary.

Luke: Right.

Scott: Once I heard this boy scream and there were monsters out of the windows, zombies.

Luke: There's no such thing as zombies.

Emerging themes

Themes that emerged from the evidence of Luke's drawing behaviours over the three years of the project were that his spontaneous 'action' representations of events and objects were not understood or valued by significant adults at home or in care/educational settings. Instead the adults wanted to teach him how to draw human figures 'realistically'. His mother was influenced by early years practitioners' perceptions of drawing in young children's development. Yet she was able to retain a reciprocal relationship with her son in drawing episodes. Luke's passion for representing images from TV and video games was shared by his mother, tolerated by his care workers and apparently not noticed by primary school staff. His love/hate relationship with scary things was shared and encouraged at home, but regarded with suspicion or 'blanked out' in pre-school and school settings. Despite his strong emotional bond with his mother, his growing sense of being a boy drew him increasingly towards the 'male' preoccupations of sport, fighting and violence, and these preoccupations were increasingly reflected in his self-chosen drawing and play activities.

5   Simon's story

Simon, 4 years 1 month, drawing at home

With his father at work and his 8-year-old sister at school, Simon spent each morning alone with his mother at the start of the project. He had been attending the nursery of the local infant school each afternoon for the last six months and was to move into the reception class at the end of the current term. Simon's mother was pleased with the amount of time he had been able to spend in what was a very popular and over-subscribed nursery class. She had some reservations about his move into the main part of the school, saying 'He only turned 4 in August. To me he's not really up to all of it'.

Drawing, for Simon, was the first activity each morning. He spent at least an hour drawing alone at the kitchen table as his mother completed household chores. We were not surprised that Simon was interested in drawing as it was highly valued within this close-knit family and went on around him all the time. Simon's mother described her husband as artistic commenting, 'He draws a lovely picture for them [the children] to colour in'. His involvement every two years in running a church activity week for teenagers coincided with the first year of the project and involved the family in making, for example, six-foot tall cardboard palm trees. Simon followed the actions of his father, copying the lettering of the club logo and drawing his own treasure hunt clues, which he hid around the house.

Simon was very particular about the paper he used for drawing and this was recognized by his mother who told us, 'It has to be a clean piece of paper every time he starts and it won't do if there's typing on the other side'. She made sure that a supply of good quality paper and drawing implements were readily available. Once completed, however, he showed little interest in his drawings, which were left stacked upon the work surface in the kitchen.

There was a lot of shared interaction between Simon and his mother in relation to drawing. Simon often asked his mother to draw things for him to colour in. She felt that her son was often frustrated as he could not achieve on paper the image which he could see in his mind, and because his older sister was able to draw more recognizable pictures than he could. In the absence of both father and sister, Simon's mother encouraged her son to learn about the effects of line, shape and colour by copying their completed artwork, which was always to hand. Simon often had one of his sister's drawings in front of him in order to produce his own version of her composition. In preparation for a visit to see Disney on Ice, for example, his sister completed a drawing of Pocahontas (Figure 5.1) and, as can be seen in Figure 5.2, Simon's version succeeds in representing key features of his sister's picture.

Figure 5.1 Pocahontas 1

Simon's mother, accepting that she was not particularly artistic, looked for further ways of supporting Simon in achieving what she termed 'a pleasing end result'. She turned to the television as an important additional source of stimuli. Mother and son watched the television programme *Art Attack* as it provided ideas and stage-by-stage direction as to how to achieve a prescribed end product. Figure 5.3, 'Flowers', is an example of the collaboration and negotiation which regularly took place between Simon and his mother. Simon's mother made the tissue paper surround and drew the outlines of the flowers which Simon then coloured in. His mother was obviously delighted with a result which reflected the programme's focus upon stereotyped and simplified cultural images. She commented 'It's quite an interesting effect isn't it?'

Simon could be very definite about what he wanted his mother to do to support him. Whereas his mother was keen to follow the stages shown in the programme in their correct order, Simon, following initial direction, often broke away from the programme's intention in order to produce his own version.

Figure 5.2 Pocahontas 2

Figure 5.3 Flowers

His mother 'tuning into' Simon's needs had learnt to accept this and to be happy with something much simpler. One example of her adjusting her behaviour was in relation to his increasing interest in football.

> We had to draw the footballers … I'd take my time and do this picture as good as I could and then he'd just colour it all in black. It would be gone and I'd think now what have you done to my footballer. So I stopped being so particular about the drawing and as long as it had a head and two legs and maybe one was kicking and two arms and shorts and a top on that was good enough – he could put the shirt colour on or whatever.

In addition to drawing, Simon enjoyed episodes of role-play structured by his very capable older sister. Common themes were 'tent making', 'hairdressers' and 'dressing up'. When his sister was at school Simon spent about three hours each day watching favourite videos or children's television programmes. He supplemented this by playing with his trains, cars and road mat, constructing elaborate traffic jams. His mother, conscious that he was spending a lot of time alone each morning, made card games, which they played together. She was keen that he would be well prepared for his move into more formal schooling and so these games usually had an educational outcome involving working with letters and numbers and keeping to rules. Although often too difficult for Simon, both he and his mother interjected a good level of humour into their playing of these games, ensuring they were enjoyable.

Simon, 4 years 1 month, drawing at nursery

The nursery Simon attended was staffed by a very experienced nursery teacher, a nursery nurse and a part-time support assistant, and had a good reputation within the local authority. The classroom was small but was divided into workshop areas and excellent use was made of the space available. The children self-selected from a wide range of provision including technology, mark making, and creative and role-play areas. Curriculum planning was based on themes or topics and we found that most of the adult directed activities that took place during the month of data collection were linked to the theme of Homes and Houses.

Simon's teacher told us that it had taken time for him to settle into his nursery class and it had been half a term before his mother could leave him. Unlike his well ordered home with its predictable routine, this was a context crammed with opportunities but also with decisions that needed to be made by him. Six months on Simon still found making choices and decisions difficult.

His teacher commented, 'His friends are two girls and if he's not involved in an activity he will look for them'. Used to female support in the home context, Simon attached himself to these confident older girls to help him through his difficulties. He had begun to tentatively enter into play with other boys when they were engaged in an activity that was familiar to him, for example with the Brio train set or construction blocks. Simon never, however, took part in their boisterous play. His teacher commented, 'He's sensible, never silly. He stands back and watches if others get too excited. Likes to please and get it right'.

Although Simon's nursery teacher recognized children's need to explore making marks on paper and the importance of drawing for developing fine motor skills, she perceived drawing as primarily supporting cognitive development. She expected that during each nursery session children would, alongside freely chosen activity, participate in one adult focussed activity. This involved 'a lot of practical activity and some recording'. Figure 5.4 is an example of Simon working within this pattern. Following an adult telling the story, *Brown Bear Brown Bear, What Do You See?* (Martin and Carle 1999) Simon was asked to retell the story three-dimensionally in the sand, using the artefacts provided and supported by an adult. Moving on to retell the story graphically (in two-dimensions), he chose white pencil and blue paper in order to create a blue horse, his favourite animal from the story. Simon

Figure 5.4   Brown bear

included a touch of humour in his representation by adding a notice next to the horse which read, 'Keep out, horses might bite'. Noticeably, given the subject matter and clear initial guidelines, Simon responded confidently and with some independence.

Simon particularly enjoyed working as part of a small group of children in the presence of an adult, carrying out an adult directed activity and talking about what he was doing. His teacher commented, 'He's open to extension and he takes it on board'. This form of interaction had much in common with his experiences of meaning making in the home context. In comparison with some of his peers, Simon was very experienced in interacting around a formal game or task. His confidence was shown in his extension of adult initiated pencil and paper activities to include the element of humour and game playing which was present in his interactions with his mother. He often adapted a completed activity, for instance, so that it became a guessing game which entertained his peers.

Given the value placed upon adult focussed activities, Simon's uncertainty when faced with initiating self-choice activity, including drawing, went largely unnoticed in the nursery context. Supported and praised by adults who encouraged him to talk about his work, made suggestions, recapped on experiences and encouraged him to add missing detail, Simon found great commonality in patterns of interaction across home and nursery. He happily fitted in with the emphasis upon representational drawing accompanied by emergent writing, which was being prioritized.

Simon, 5 years 1 month, drawing at home

When we returned to Simon one year later, it was obvious that he had grown greatly in confidence. His physical, emotional and social well being was reflected in his opinion of himself as a drawer and in his ability to represent his own ideas through drawing. One example of this was when we asked whether he ever needed his mother's help when drawing and he replied, 'No, there's always something else I can do on my own'. Contributing factors to what Dweck (1986) would consider as Simon's 'mastery approach' to drawing were his increased physical strength and dexterity and the opportunity to compare his own performance favourably with those of his male peers within the school context. At home his 9-year-old sister's lack of interest in drawing now that she spent her time on music lessons, Brownies and homework, and his mother's purchase of specialist art materials for him to work with, reinforced his perception of his importance as an artist.

Simon's father had spent the summer convalescing at home following an illness and Simon had certainly benefited from this. It coincided with the televising of the World Cup and Simon's father became a willing participant in his son's challenges to 'draw or copy your favourite footballer'. We sympathized with his mother who was placed in the unenviable position of having to judge between two equally competitive males, knowing that neither would take being the runner up well!

Whilst both mother and father would sit and draw alongside Simon, at his request, he was no longer interested in copying from them. The 'joint involvement episodes' (Schaffer 1992), which took place between Simon and his father, focussed upon drawing and were a particularly important influence upon Simon's interest and developing expertise. Simon's father found playful ways of introducing Simon to shading, perspective and more advanced pencil skills, without having a negative effect upon his confidence. Drawing alongside Simon, he encouraged him to evaluate his own drawings by talking critically about his own. When considering his observational drawing of the new bicycle he had received for his fifth birthday (Figure 5.5) Simon commented, 'Good try on the metal bits'.

Simon's dual passions of football and drawing could be seen in the numerous drawings which related to the football theme. His football annuals were important stimuli for the form of presentation he used. His mother discussed with us the frustration of a 5-year-old with high standards struggling with problems of proportion as he tried to copy his favourite images. 'The other day he started Carlsberg, but he started too big so it wasn't all

Figure 5.5 Bicycle

going to fit on with a gap at the other side of the shirt. Well it isn't good enough for him. He won't finish it because it's not right.' As a 5-year-old, Simon, imbued with a general sense of well being and a strong belief in himself as a drawer, seemed to find the tasks he set himself challenging, but not daunting. His enthusiasm for drawing seemed unlimited and new plans were made for drawings at night in bed, which were carried out before school the next day.

Simon's favourite drawing was of his football hero David Beckham (Figure 5.6). In this drawing he used various sources as stimuli. These included a black and white print of Beckham from his football book, the banner headlines of his annuals, his detailed knowledge of team colours and badges and a new fascination with drawing dramatic faces. The phrase, 'Beckham has a full

Figure 5.6 David Beckham

head of confidence and always goes up for high tackles' was written from memory above this drawing. Its origin was unknown but it had obviously captured Simon's imagination.

Simon's mother was happy to encourage his interest in football and drew attention to his increased interest in recognizing numbers and letters because of their presence on football shirts. She was less happy with his copying of images and phrases from the advertising of the *Star Wars* film on cereal boxes and collectors stickers (Figure 5.7). For her *Star Wars* was 'a wretched thing'. She complained about the amount of publicity there had been for the film during the summer commenting, 'You couldn't go to any of the fast food places without them giving something away'. The phrases copied by Simon to accompany images of, for example, the character Darth Maul included

Figure 5.7 *Star Wars*

'ominous and brooding', 'menacing and powerful' and 'striking fear into those who oppose him'. These phrases had little place for Simon's mother in the home context, but were seen to be part of the superhero play which she recognized now took place at school during playtimes. Certainly the drawings brought home by Simon from school each day had a football or *Star Wars* theme.

During the second year of the project Simon spent most of his time drawing, playing at schools or post offices with his older sister at home or watching videoed football matches. Although watching the television was usually his first activity after a day at school and part of a 'winding down' process, his mother noticed that watching football was now regularly interspersed with 'kicking the football up and down' in the garden, the kitchen and through the hall, shouting footballers' names and repeating, 'What a pass'. As in Marsh's (2002) study of much younger children, Simon used the stimulus of television to play out and develop his own narratives. Simon's mother did not expect him to have a particular friend at school that could be invited home to play as she did with his sister. She commented, 'I don't think boys do it the same'. There was little opportunity for Simon to play with other children as those who lived nearby either went to a different school or were considered by Simon's mother to be the wrong age. In any case Simon and his sister were not allowed to play out on the street.

Simon, 5 years 1 month, Year One, school context

At 5 years and 1 month Simon was the youngest of ten Year One children in a mixed Year One/Year Two class. He had spent two terms in the nursery and the reception class. His teacher commented upon the impact of trying to meet the statutory requirements of the Key Stage One curriculum, 'We now have a timetable in order to fit every subject in, with very little time for free choice'. In comparison with the 'integrated day' she found whole class teaching, 'Much easier to manage and much easier to ensure that the children had covered everything'. She added, however, that in comparison with the time prior to the introduction of the literacy hour, she now had little time to talk to individuals as she was constantly teaching. The teacher felt it was necessary to heavily direct children's activity and there was a lack of provision for children as independent or collaborative learners in the planning and organization of activities. With a new class and in the 'run up' to an Ofsted inspection, the statutory weekly art lesson was not a priority and there is no evidence collected of art work completed during this period. The teacher accepted that art, as a foundation subject, 'took a back seat'.

In spite of this it appeared that Simon was thriving. The pattern of learning set down for Simon in the home context had been adult structured activity and seated paper and pencil work, often in the company of an older, academically able sibling. Given this, Simon did not find the daily routine of the Key Stage One classroom restrictive. We could see a commonality of experience across home and school which was fostering in Simon a sense of well being.

This well being was supported by Simon's teacher. Although preoccupied with the demands of prescribed curriculum delivery, Simon's teacher tolerated with humour his ability to adapt and give a football theme to many of the activities he was required to complete. She observed, 'He doesn't talk a lot, but when he does talk he will talk about football'. Recognizing that all the boys in her class were 'football orientated' she brought a football book of her own into the classroom which Simon regularly chose to read. Figure 5.8 is an example of one of the many drawings completed at the end of a lesson when, if the class finished set work early, they could 'read, write or draw'. It is not surprising that Simon chose to draw or that his drawings related to football.

Simon was stimulated by the presence of the older children and spent a lot of time watching them in the classroom. On the playground, however, he stayed with the other Year One boys in his class. During 'wet playtimes' Simon was unusual amongst his male peers in not choosing the boy-dominated construction area in which to play. Seemingly confident in his

Figure 5.8 Footballers

sense of self, at every available opportunity he chose to draw. Wet playtime drawings were completed alone or with one other similar minded boy. Simon did, however, conform to what Paley (1986a: ix) terms 'the five-year-old's passion for segregation by sex' in choosing not to sit with the girls who grouped together in order to draw.

Simon, 6 years 1 month, Year Two, home context

As we returned for the final time to talk to Simon and his mother, she told us that she was worrying about him in his new class. She felt he was not coping in his Year Two class and knew he was worrying about the numeracy lesson which, alongside the Literacy Hour, dominated each morning. Because of this she was allowing him to miss school occasionally when he complained of stomach ache saying, 'He's not having an easy time really. He doesn't like the work'. Having an August birthday she felt he would have gained more confidence by being placed in the class that contained only Year One children. Over a two-year period, between the ages of 4 and 6, Simon had spent time in four different classes. Apart from his time in nursery, having an August birthday he had been the youngest in each class. With hindsight, his mother felt that the school's decision-making process regarding the placing of Simon seemed to have prioritized his academic competency rather than his social and emotional needs.

It was unsurprising that Simon was exhausted after a day at school and that some of the enthusiasm, confidence and sense of well being, present during the previous year, seemed to be missing. We were surprised, however, given his total absorption with drawing when aged 5, that he was making very little use of drawing in the home context. The only drawings completed were either traced or relied upon the instructions of others and they drew heavily upon media images. Simon, as in the first year of our project, needed support in knowing what to do and how to get started. Figure 5.9 is typical of the kind of drawing Simon was producing and is his attempt to follow instructions from the book *How to Draw Disney Characters*. Simon was shown how to divide the page and fit lines into the space available in order to recreate the image shown in the book.

In contrast, Figure 5.10 of robots seems to have been completed with greater energy. This drawing was collected by Simon's mother, but was completed by Simon at school, as he found a few moments to work alongside his friend Steven, another drawer. Simon's mother spoke of Simon's growing interest in robots through watching *Robot Wars* on television. 'It's something they can draw that's intricate . . . It has this strength and all these noughts to show how strong its going to be.' As they drew, the two boys competed to create the strongest robot.

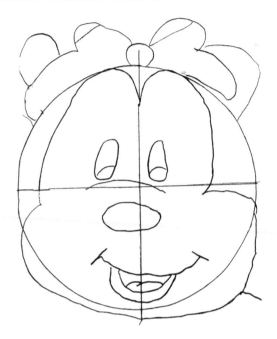

Figure 5.9 Disney character

Figure 5.10 Robot Wars

In her efforts to support Simon, his mother encouraged his attempts to create some of the three-dimensional representations modelled on the television programme *Blue Peter* and he particularly enjoyed making a cardboard box table football. She had also introduced him to 'stories with chapters' and he enjoyed having a chapter read to him each evening. As a result of this and his growing ability to write unaided, he had begun to write a novel on the home computer, returning regularly to draft additional chapters.

Simon, 6 years 1 month, Year Two, school context

During the final year of the project, Simon was an anxious child in his school setting. This contrasted markedly with the contentment and mastery orientation demonstrated in his mixed Year One and Year Two class. The move into a high ability streamed class of Year Two children had proved difficult for Simon. Certainly much was expected of him as an academically capable child in a school year that was dominated by SATs. A sensitive child, Simon now viewed school very seriously but showed little enthusiasm for any part of the daily routine.

In comparison with his previous teacher, who was experienced, relaxed and very aware of Simon as her youngest child, his new teacher was unfamiliar to both the school and to Simon and had trained to teach Key Stage Two children. Having been seconded to the infant school from the junior school where she had taught children in Year Four she admitted to having over-estimated the level at which she set literacy and numeracy work during the early weeks of the new term. The stress this caused Simon was further compounded by his physical context. His portable classroom was virtually a self-contained unit, situated near to the junior school. Being 'housed' in this building restricted Simon's contact with the warm and familiar main school to mainly whole class assembly times, and he missed the opportunities he might have had to be a relatively 'big fish in a small pool'.

Opportunities to draw were an important part of the QCA Art and Design and Technology schemes of work being used by his teacher. Despite a lack of training opportunities in art education, Simon's teacher seemed confident as she talked to us about her approach to the weekly art lesson.

> Fourteen was the age when I last had any art lessons. I know I'm not a very good artist, I make that clear to the children. I'll model something to show them. I have the whole class on the carpet and I've an object in front of us and I'll show them exactly bit by bit what I'm doing.

The task of drawing of an apple from observation, featured in Figure 5.11, should have been enjoyable for Simon, given his familiarity with the terms

Figure 5.11   Apple

'shading' and 'sketching' which were introduced within the lesson. Simon responded very seriously to what was asked of him, being anxious to grasp what the teacher required of him and what would make the activity a success. Any pleasure in drawing seemed to be overshadowed by his general lack of confidence. His teacher commented, 'I don't think he's overly confident at all. I think he can feel quite insecure sometimes'. This insecurity was also evident in his completion of a plan for the puppet he would make in design and technology shown in Figure 5.12. He had particular difficulty in making sense of the overall aim of the puppet theme as it was spread out over a series of weekly lessons. Just as he had in his nursery context, Simon found 'getting started' very difficult and was particularly concerned when his teacher asked him to start the activity over again because he had not properly understood the task.

Within a 'packed' timetable Simon's teacher explained that she could only find 30 minutes time each Friday afternoon when her children could take part in freely chosen activity. Because of this, playtimes spent indoors were particularly important to Simon. Outdoor play times were proving dif- ficult as, unlike his male peers, Simon lacked the 'coping' skills they had built up as they regularly played with other boys out of the school context. Recognition by his peers was becoming increasingly important for Simon's social and emotional welfare. He spoke to his mother about the small 'gang' of boys he played with saying, 'I'm not listened to because I'm the youngest'.

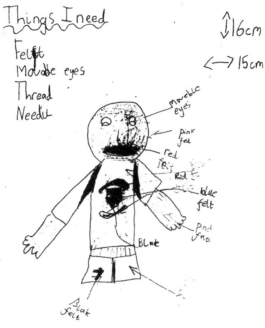

Figure 5.12 Puppet plan

In contrast, indoor playtimes were a time when Simon felt he was a valued member of his male peer group.

Each indoor playtime saw Simon gathering together with a small group of boys to design and make a large football poster. Despite much work going into the bold-lettered names of the two teams across the top of the page, the poster was never finished. The starting of a new one each indoor playtime was evidence of the boys' ongoing preoccupation with this activity and Simon played a full part in the group planning process, which seemed to be the most important part of what they did. The depth of discussion which took place within this activity surprised the teacher as such a level of involvement was not characteristic of their behaviour during teacher planned and directed lessons. The fascinations children held in common had failed to become part of the curriculum and the opportunity to bring together the developing separation of school culture and children's own culture, through informal shared dialogue around drawing, was being lost in the school context.

Summary

Across the three years of the study, Simon's drawing development was influenced by the value and support given to it as an activity in the home context by his parents. Unlike other children in the study, there was little competition in terms of other forms of meaning making. Both the interest of his father in what his mother termed 'artistic activity', and Simon's fascination with televized football, were fundamental to the progress Simon made in making meaning through graphic form. However, as he broke away from the dominance of the stereotypical images emphasized by his well meaning mother, the importance of striving for realistic representation was encouraged in all contexts. Whilst he found it hard to take advantage of the opportunities for free choice and independent play afforded in his nursery setting, he also had difficulty in living up to what he perceived were the expectations of his Year Two class teacher. He seemed happiest and most confident in his drawing ability as a very young 5-year-old in the mixed Year One and Year Two class. This was where the balance of direction and freedom most closely matched his experiences in the home context.

6 Holly's story

Holly, 4 years 6 months, drawing at home

Holly was the oldest of three children at the start of our project. She had a 3-year-old brother and a 1-year-old sister. Her mother was at home full time and her father, a shift worker, also spent a great deal of time with the children. The extended family, especially the grandparents, figured strongly in family routines and rituals. All were committed Christians and many family activities were associated with church events. Holly's mother and father had made a conscious decision that the television would not be watched until after eight o'clock when the children were asleep. This was a gentle and relaxed household where interactions between family members reflected the leisurely pace with which the day unfolded. The children were listened to and their questions were responded to with care.

The lounge, which ran from the front to the back of the house, was used by the family as both a living room and a play room, and was full of young children's toys. After attending nursery each morning, Holly spent the rest of the day in either free play or helping her mother with household tasks. Her mother remembered needing to be involved in her own mother's tasks when she was Holly's age. 'I can see a lot of me in Holly because I always wanted to do jobs with our Mam, offer to make the beds, wash up and Mam taught me to bake when I was 9 and I can imagine her to be like that.' Storying was a part of every day routine. Stories were requested by Holly about when her mother or father were little, or were invented by Holly's father telling of simple moral dilemmas faced by animal characters. Holly often asked her father to draw and label these characters for her.

Although Holly enjoyed helping her mother, it was to her father that she turned for play episodes. He involved both Holly and her brother in three-dimensional construction activities, making boats and aeroplanes with Stickle bricks. Holly was a willing partner in these episodes. Whilst she accepted her father and grandparents as play partners, Holly and her brother excluded their mother saying she was 'not good enough' and she accepted this. When playing without an adult present Holly could often shut out the younger children and concentrate on her personal play agenda. She used her two favourite dolls to replicate domestic scenes and routines, and collected objects, mainly toys, to set out as, for instance, elaborate birthday teas.

Whereas as a 3-year-old she had set out shops, her current arrangements reflected her recent attendance at a range of birthday parties.

Each Sunday, following attendance at church, Holly visited her maternal grandmother. In the context of her grandmother's house, where children's drawing was particularly valued, Holly was a prolific drawer. Confirming Malchiodi's (1998) recognition of the importance of the influence of the immediate environment upon drawing, Holly's participation in drawing activity was supported by the plentiful supply of paper, always available in a designated area of the living room. All the grandchildren accessed this paper and, when Holly was younger, her older male cousins had been role models for drawing behaviours. For the children drawing was the only 'play' activity on offer and Holly rapidly completed many sequences of drawings. Adults praised and accepted her drawings without making suggestions for improvement. Holly, strongly independent in any case, usually rejected offers of help, annoyed that an adult's interference might cause a picture to be spoilt. Help with drawing had to be requested by Holly, rather than being offered by others. Her father told us that when she was first drawing she would say 'Draw me a face, Dad' or 'Draw me an elephant, Dad, or a dog' and that she would try and copy it. He recalled that as he drew he had been honest with Holly saying, 'Dad's not very good at drawing'.

Holly's drawings were autobiographical, being linked to her or her family's everyday or recollected experiences. Many represented the family at home or church and showed Holly's particular fascination with the topological layout of rooms. Just as her three-dimensional arrangements completed at home included many objects and small figures spread across the floor, so her mapped out drawings were crammed with figures. Many figures were undifferentiated and schematic but occasionally a key figure had additional detail that made him or her recognizable. A Sunday school teacher in her representation of Sunday school shown in Figure 6.1 was drawn with 'teeth and guitar'. These were salient features both of his appearance and his role at church which dominated Holly's visual remembering. She also accurately represented, from memory, clearly delineated areas for adult worship, Sunday school and socializing. Holly's drawing activity was characterized by its fluidity as on page after page she replayed everyday experiences. Figure 6.2 sums up her visual impression of her first visit to the main infant school in preparation for her imminent move into the reception class. For Holly the large television, high on top of a cupboard, the 'church-like' windows and the large teacher's table dominated her visual memories.

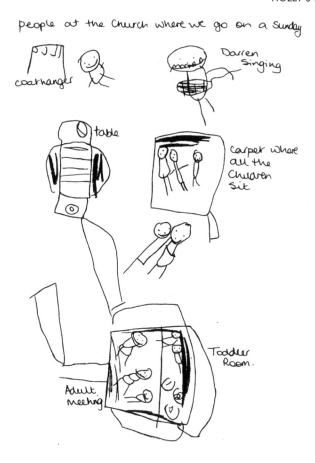

people at the Church where we go on a Sunday

coathanger

Darren Singing

table

Carpet where all the Children sit

Adult meeting

Toddler Room.

Figure 6.1 Sunday school

Holly 4 years 6 months, drawing at nursery

Holly attended the same nursery class as Simon and, like him, would move to the main school in a few months time. Most of the children spent two terms in the nursery before they moved into the main infant school and were therefore between 4 and 5 years old. Their very competent nursery teacher recognized that all adults working with the children within the nursery ought to share a common philosophy and a common understanding of the values and aims which underpinned planned activities. She introduced her staff to the key teaching points and the forms of interaction that might be used by modelling for them the role the adult should take in any new activity.

Holly was seen by the nursery teacher as quiet but purposeful. 'She has a

Figure 6.2 Visit to school

purpose whatever area she goes into … She's able to develop her own thinking by using the artefacts but she's also good at using an adult as a resource … if there's anything she wants to know, she's not worried about asking.' Holly's confidence in graphic representation, developed particularly at her grandmother's home, was obvious. She chose, more often than other children, to record graphically if interested in a theme and seemed to follow through the adult-led pattern of input, followed by three-dimensional activity and two-dimensional recording, without needing adult prompts. Given the constant linking of adult activity and talk to the half-termly nursery theme of Houses and Homes, it was unsurprising that the content of Holly's child-chosen drawing activity, collected during the month, related to the same theme.

Figure 6.3 is Holly's drawn response following the completion of a focus activity in the wet sand. Following adult modelling of the activity, Holly had used artefacts placed in the sand to plan her route from home to the nursery. The drawing was self-initiated and completed in the writing area later that morning. Holly discussed the finished drawing in great detail with a nearby adult who, following common nursery practice, labelled parts of the drawing identified by Holly within her 'storying'. Even at pre-school, Holly was receiving constant messages about the importance and dominance of writing as a symbol system.

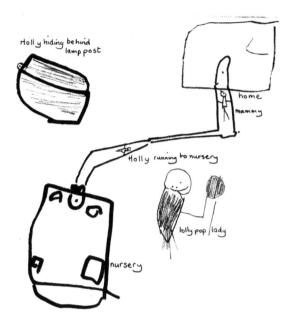

Figure 6.3 Route from home to nursery

Most of Holly's drawings collected in the nursery setting seemed to have been completed with greater care and contained a little more detail than those completed at home. They also, however, seemed more restrained, lacking the fluency, energy and spontaneity of drawings completed at home or particularly at Holly's grandmother's. There was a sense that Holly was 'keeping in mind' the instructions of others and was conscious of the need for a finished product that met adult requirements. Certainly in the nursery setting the 'school' agenda, where adults determined the pattern and to some extent the content of activities, would seem to have constrained Holly's opportunities to represent, through graphic media, her own interests. Some three weeks later, when adult focus activities had moved on from the 'journey to school' theme, Holly completed Figure 6.4, which is a far more free and fluid response to the same theme and is the result of Holly linking the nursery theme to her own lived experience.

In the nursery, Holly happily took part in the full range of adult initiated activities. Her self-chosen activities, however, usually took place within the particularly well provisioned role-play or construction areas and could therefore be seen to echo those that took place in the home context. She was content to work alone through play scripts linked to the daily routine of mother and baby and was supported in this by miniature realistic props. Her interaction with her peers was differentiated according to their age and sex.

Figure 6.4 Running to nursery

She was interested in the actions of older girls in the role-play area, but although she watched them closely as she worked alongside them, she did not change her own play script. She avoided working with same age or older boys in the block area, however, preferring to wait until they had left before she entered. In common with her play in the home setting, she was able to 'block out' younger children, working alongside but virtually ignoring them. When an adult gave her responsibility for encouraging a younger child, however, she was caring of them and was able to support their play. Holly was already being cast both at home and school in the role of female 'carer'.

Holly, 5 years 6 months, drawing at home

One year later, and Holly was 'big sister' to another baby boy. She had just moved into a Year One class and her mother had prepared her by saying, 'You won't be able to play quite as much you know but there still will be things to play'. Her mother commented on the difference for children as they moved from reception to Year One and recognized that Holly would miss having dolls to play with.

Precious time for play in the home context was now taken up with 'homework', set by school. It was Holly's mother who ensured that reading or

writing tasks were completed and this led to some difficulty in their relationship. She was sure Holly tried harder at school and was lazy at home.
Although Holly enjoyed looking at books on her own and having stories read
to her, she told us of her dislike of reading the books she brought home from
school saying, 'I don't like reading ... When I've got a new school book I have
to read it. My Mam gets it out and she wants me to do it but I don't want to do
it'.

Although Holly enjoyed writing and was beginning to incorporate it into
her drawings as lists or labels for the members of her family, Holly had been
criticized by her teacher during parents' evening for rushing her work and not
forming her letters properly. Her mother, who had practised letter formation
with Holly at home, knew she could form her letters correctly and commented, 'At home I will say "Do it nice and slowly, take your time" and she
will do it perfectly'. Interaction around reading and writing seemed to be
casting Holly to some extent in a deficit role. As the oldest child in the family
who had constantly been reminded of her practical capability this must have
challenged her self-image as a 'school' learner.

Holly's preoccupations and interests centred upon the female role. Her
identification with her mother's role continued and she regularly followed
her into the kitchen complaining that she wasn't allowed to do enough to
help her. Holly's mother and father, having sponsored a little girl of Holly's
age from Zimbabwe, had described to Holly how she would not have many
toys and that she would be expected to help her mother a lot, particularly as
she had a new baby. Holly strongly identified with this little girl and wanted
to do everything she could to help her own mother. Her mother commented,
'She is ironing and all sorts if I let her'.

The influence of her female peers at school was now becoming evident in
the home context. Holly rarely played with boys and when she was invited to
play at her friends' houses after school, she came home talking of Barbies,
having acted out scenarios with the teen figures. When girls came to her
house to play, her mother talked of them 'swapping shoes and things'. Holly's
mother recognized her daughter's growing awareness of fashion and her
visual appearance saying, 'She often talks about the twins because she wants
her hair like theirs, a long plait down the back, so she is growing her hair'.
Bedtime, a favourite time of the day for Holly when she felt particularly close
to her mother, was a time for sharing stories of everyday events. Holly
favourite stories were her mother's recollections of being a teenager.

Although the television was rarely turned on, the children had phases
when they watched videos, inherited from family and friends. Holly's choice
of Pocahontas as her favourite video and her preference for the music of
Shania Twain, heard on the radio and sung along to by mother and daughter,
confirmed her interest in female role models. Holly rejected *Superman*, her
brother's favourite video, leaving him to watch it alone.

Whist still playing with dolls, Holly now adopted the roles of both mother and teacher within her play scripts by giving both her dolls, Christopher and Sophie, bottles and reading books as she set them out on the settee before breakfast.

Although one year earlier Holly's visits to her grandmother's house had stimulated drawing activity, she now drew constantly at home as well and the combined output made her a prolific drawer. In contrast with the pressured interaction around homework, interaction around drawing remained relaxed, with Holly continuing to receive unconditional praise. Her rapidly completed autobiographical pictures focussed upon members of her family in everyday situations and Figure 6.5, showing, 'Lots of people doing different things', is typical of many of these drawings. Holly represented her grandmother as 'Nana with babies in her tummy', drawing upon the fascination she had with the story of the birth of her twin uncles.

Figure 6.6 was Holly's favourite drawing and depicts, 'A house with hearts and stars and things on it.' Although completed at home, it was typical of the decorative drawings Holly completed when seated with her female peers at school. Holly began with a static image of a house or a girl and built up patterning around them. Her mother commented, 'She learnt to draw hearts and that's it, she draws hearts on everything ... I look in her reading bag and she will have what I would call a girly picture now with the eyes and eyelashes and the sun and the sky and the grass'. When asked about the 'high heels' of both the male and female images she drew Holly said this was because, 'Princes in story books have high heels'. Certainly her re-reading of available story books at home, for example Cinderella, the Goose Girl and Snow White and the Seven Dwarfs presented her with such images.

Holly, 5 years 6 months, drawing at school

As Holly's mother had warned, there was no opportunity in school in Year One for Holly to continue her enjoyment of using dolls and found objects to re-enact her internal narratives. In class, Holly was a quiet but enthusiastic child, who talked one-to-one very happily but did not seek attention. She listened carefully both to the instructions given by adults and to the conversations of her female peers.

Holly's school day was now dominated by teacher initiated activity and the constraints of fitting into each morning both a literacy hour and the newly introduced numeracy lesson. Holly's teacher had taught a reception class the previous year and had a background of working with 4-year-old children. She felt that moving away from an 'integrated day' to subject specific lessons was particularly hard for the children at the beginning of Year One. She felt that ideally they should have 'a lot more opportunities to be

Nana with babies in her tummy

Holly eat sweets

Katy having a drink

Andy playing

baby Leigh crawling

Figure 6.5 Family

Figure 6.6 House with hearts and stars

involved in role play and to develop their own ideas and socialize'. Although she tried to cover the statutory curriculum through practical activities, she felt that she was often 'pushing them through hoops' rather than encouraging them to become involved in an activity over a length of time. Her comments drew attention to the lack of priority being given to these young children's interests and preoccupations. 'Sometimes if a child has completed a task I will give them a limited choice about what they can do after that, but often it wouldn't be until towards the end of an afternoon that they would have half an hour, say on a Friday.' The strict timetabling of the day had an impact on the arrangement of the classroom and the availability of resources. Across all the Year One classes in the school, role-play areas had been disbanded, along with sand and water provision and purpose built technology tables. Holly's teacher justified the domination of space by tables and chairs by the expectation that for the majority of the day the children would be seated. She seemed helpless as she commented on these unwelcome changes, 'I couldn't believe it, what they had come from, the richness of the reception class and the environment and to come into Year One . . .' The prioritizing of literacy and numeracy ensured the computer had a prominent place within the classroom and that the writing centre was retained. The small-scale construction kits, only available upon finishing teacher directed tasks or during wet playtimes, were retained because they could fit on table tops. This provision, alongside 'read, write or draw' had a powerful effect upon the form children's meaning making took within the classroom.

Holly's teacher commented that she had noticed a gender difference in the children's ability to cope with the pencil and paper orientated day. 'Generally the boys get tired more quickly and they are the ones who want to be into construction as soon as they finish an activity.' Unlike her male peers, Holly's choice of 'free time' activity did not include construction. The boys' domination of the construction area had increased as they moved through the reception class and into Year One and Holly had learned that this activity was not available to her. A combination of 'talk and draw' therefore became a substitute for the missing role-play area. Girls seated themselves in increasingly large groups around tables and, both orally and graphically, explored their growing fascination with the themes of love, friendship and what Holly's mother termed the 'girly decorations' of hair ornaments, jewellery and shoes. By Year One there was a seeming acceptance by teacher and children that these drawings were part of the separate or 'unofficial' school peer culture, identified by Pollard (1996) as a central feature of children's 'school' worlds. This female drawing community held little status in teachers' eyes and within the school environment.

In theory, drawing was available to Holly in three forms: the self-chosen drawings completed with female peers during wet playtimes or when teacher directed tasks were complete; drawing as part of teacher directed tasks which supported a range of curriculum areas; and drawing as part of the weekly art lesson. As a foundation subject, art lessons were timetabled as 50-minute sessions one afternoon each week. In practice, however, as the school prepared for an Ofsted inspection, the teacher admitted that the current 'official' art lesson consisted of 'trying to get lots of groups through a printing activity' in order to complete a display.

Figure 6.7 is typical of the drawings that were collected by Holly's teacher. It shows Holly's completion of a pre-printed format with a decorative border, which invited Holly to draw and write a sentence within a particular space. This was part of the ongoing religious education topic of friendship. Many of the stereotypical patterns used as borders, for example hearts and flowers, would have appealed to the girls in the class but would have had little appeal or credibility for the boys. Holly used many of these low-level recording activities to continue her preoccupation with figure drawing, though often frustrated by limited access to drawing materials dominated by 'clumsy' wax crayons and blunt pencils. Over the one-month period of data collection, Holly's book contained 11 drawings. One was a wet-playtime drawing and ten conformed to subject matter decided by the teacher. Of those ten, five were heavily structured by a pre-delineated space.

Figure 6.7 Friendship

Holly, 6 years 6 months, drawing at home

By the third year of the project in order to accommodate their ever-growing family, Holly's mother and father had carried out extensive building work on their home. This enabled Holly to have her own 'Barbie-themed' bedroom and to have some time away from the demands of the younger children. Pride of place in Holly's bedroom was her desk where she played 'schools'. Holly still played with her brothers and sister but being the oldest was not always easy. She was used to taking the lead in play and was seen by her mother as having a tendency to be 'bossy'. Faced with Holly's tears when her brother's and sister's friends escaped from their role as her 'audience', Holly's mother had to explain to her eldest daughter the necessity for give and take in relationships with others.

Holly continued to make a distinction between her dislike of reading schoolbooks and her enjoyment of story-books at home. Her mother, reassured by the school that Holly's reading had improved and was now average, continued to help her daughter with 'formal' literacy. They had come to an agreement that she would sit with Holly straight after school and 'do her book' and then let her go off to play. If she came to her parents later in the evening and asked for help with reading they always said yes. This was working well. Holly knew that once the set reading was completed, she had control over any additional reading.

Holly's parents had also tried to change Holly's hurried and careless approach to writing. Her father constantly reminded her of the need for it to be 'neater and nicer'. Holly's mother felt that this strategy had worked. Commenting on Holly's writing she told us, 'She's always in such a rush to get it done ... She did say if she took her time it would take her so long, she wouldn't get it finished ... and I think she thought the teacher might be cross with her'. There seemed to be a conflict for Holly between the need to carry out tasks well and the need to finish within the prescribed time limits she was given in the school context. Holly was unable to conform to the dual expectation that she should complete set work both quickly and neatly.

Holly's parents had decided not to renew their television licence as they watched television so little. The radio was no longer enough for Holly, however, and she, very unusually, asked to stay for tea at her cousin's house in order to see for herself the dance routines which older girls were imitating when outside at playtimes. Visits to her best friend Elizabeth's house had also increased. Elizabeth had a television and video in her room and the two girls watched Disney videos about Ariel, a cartoon mermaid. Her mother commented that following that 'she got really into it and she had a book about it'. Figure 6.8 shows one of the many representations of mermaids, which Holly drew following watching and 'acting out' the female role in the video.

Figure 6.8 *Little Mermaid*

Holly's mother supported her daughter's role-play by finding a long pink dress in a charity shop. Holly loved this dress and used it to sing along to her own video of *The Swan Princess* taking the main role of Odette.

When playing with her brothers and sister, Holly continued to set out found objects. She now, however, incorporated Barbies and a disco into the themes of tea parties when playing with her 3-year-old sister. Role-play with her oldest brother, now aged 5, had a strong narrative theme. Although they still used complex arrangements of objects, they also included themselves as key figures within the script. Holly's mother recounted a play script integrating several story themes, taking account of the particular interests of each child and the preparations for Christmas which were beginning all around them.

> In the night Holly and her brother were the big giants. Every night they would come and make stuff for the little people. Soon the house was knocked down and the big giant would build it again. The little mermaid people would swim to the homes and say hello and the people would talk to the mermaids. The big giants would make the wind and blow the house down. The Father Christmas would come on the night and give them slides and toys.

Although willing to spend time playing with her younger siblings, Holly spent a great deal of time alone. Apart from video inspired drawings of mermaids, Holly repeatedly drew side views of a bride and groom declaring their love for each other. Figure 6.9, drawn for her parents, is complete with the speech bubbles that had been introduced to her in the school context. It also contains the 'tears of joy', which were part of the fairy tales Holly now read to herself. Holly's mother felt these drawings were inspired by Holly's fascination with her parents' wedding and the wedding photograph which was prominently displayed in the lounge.

Figure 6.9 To Mammy and Daddy

Holly, 6 years 6 months, drawing at school

In a Year Two class in the final year in the infant school, Holly was being prepared for the end of Key Stage One statutory assessments. The Year Two children had been 'streamed' in preparation for SATs coaching. Holly was unconcerned saying, 'As long as I have Elizabeth I'm not really bothered'.

Her new teacher was very capable, experienced and efficient. She felt that prior to the introduction of the literacy hour and numeracy lesson there had been opportunities to give the children experience of working with different media. In comparison, art activities were now far more structured. 'Now I feel as though I am actually teaching children the skills which before I think would just happen by chance ... I think we're far more focussed as far as learning objectives now and the reason for doing activities ... there are more steps to it.'

The term's art work included line drawing and colour mixing, and was also linked to an ICT topic which was a drawing programme. Figure 6.10 shows Holly's response to the teacher's request that the children tried out an activity on paper that she had modelled for them on the computer. The teacher regularly used modelling as a strategy for showing the effect she was trying to achieve. She felt the children needed guidance but then needed to

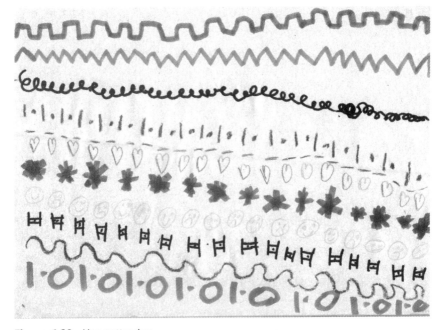

Figure 6.10 Line patterning

be left alone when completing the activity. She encouraged sketching with lots of attempts on one page and self-evaluation, 'Try it lots of times and see which one you feel's the best ... If you think it's good then it's good'.

All Holly's drawings collected in the school context were directed and modelled by an adult prior to her starting them. As in the previous year, Holly took every opportunity to accommodate her own interests. In Figure 6.11, which depicts the correct use of medicine, a drug awareness theme becomes a

Figure 6.11 Drug awareness

vehicle once again for Holly to draw a decorative female figure. Holly's mother recovered a drawing from the bottom of her school bag shown in Figure 6.12. It was a refined and further developed version of the 'marriage' theme. This image, constantly depicted during the previous year, had been completed and developed once more with female peers during a wet playtime. Wet playtimes appeared to be the only opportunities the children had for self-initiated drawing activities in school.

Summary

In the home context Holly was independent and determined. She maintained dual forms of meaning making across the three years of the study. As a 6-year-old,

Figure 6.12 Decorative figures

her 'acting out' of the narratives of lead female video heroines supplemented and eventually overtook 'setting out' of objects. Her use of drawing, however, remained constant and prolific. During the school day, her time was dominated by the need to fit into the routines and rituals of the educational agenda. As she moved from the foundation stage into Key Stage One, wet playtimes afforded her the opportunity to use drawing within a social agenda predominantly with girl friends.

7 Lianne's story

Lianne 5 years, drawing at home

Lianne was the oldest child taking part in the project. Her mother, a classroom assistant at her school, understood the rites and rituals of both home and school settings and was therefore well placed to provide for her daughter's meaning making across both contexts. Lianne's brother Tom, who was two years older, was a quiet and gentle boy. His mother encouraged him to fit in with his sister's needs, particularly in relation to her play agenda.

Lianne's home was untidy, slightly chaotic, warm and accepting. Her mother had a very positive outlook on life and delighted in her daughter. She was always ready to accommodate her extended role-play scripts. She encouraged her husband and son to take Lianne's play seriously. She told of the fatal mistake they made in 'drop kicking the doll' as part of an impromptu game of indoor football. Lianne's outrage, backed up by her mother, soon put a stop to that kind of behaviour. 'Well I told them off . . . You haven't to do that because she really loves the babies.' After being taken to task, Lianne's father, in the role of grandfather, held the babies when Lianne instructed him to do so. 'She wraps the babies in shawls and says "Grandad you'll have to mind the baby" . . . and they're all part of it now.' On Sundays father and son went down to the club before Sunday dinner, leaving mother and daughter to 'do things together'. After dinner, all four sat down to play board games together.

In confirmation of the views of both Malchiodi (1998) and Pahl (2002) about the importance of combining modes of play without constraints, Lianne was supported by her mother's relaxed attitude to the use of home space. Lianne's role-play was given both space and time. Her mother accepted her need to gather and rearrange everyday found objects. Six weeks into being a 'pupil', Figure 7.1 shows Lianne celebrating her delight in the new culture of schooling into which she had been inducted. Her bedroom was set out for long periods as a school and, to accommodate this, Lianne was allowed to sleep in her brother's bedroom. Her mother reported:

> She's made a classroom in her bedroom and she's stayed there – it must have been three and a half hours yesterday. It took shape on Sunday morning because I'd put a little desk in, moved out of her

Figure 7.1 Teaching dolls

brother's room. She's got all her paper in and her crayons, and when I went up she said, 'Can we have a meeting so I can tell you what the kids have done?' That's me on a Monday morning. She has to sit there while I go to the staff meeting. But I was busy and when I went in she was reading a story, pretending to read. . . all the teddy bears and everything lined up – unbelievable.

Drawing was generally used to support Lianne's role-play with pens, pencils and paper in plentiful supply and freely available. She had already learnt that good drawing was about accurate representation. She reported to us Lianne's irritation over the past 12 months 'because we didn't used to know what the drawings were. But anyway she did'. Her mother made it clear that she herself was not good at drawing but was willing to help her when she got frustrated. 'If she can't do a proper shape like a ball she gets upset, so, if it was a ball I'd get a circle and say "Why don't you draw around this?"' Her brother, Tom, was expected to model both drawing and writing for his sister and took pride in her successes: 'He thinks they [her drawings] are beautiful and if she does something he thinks is really good he gets excited and says, "Lianne's done this".'

Lianne 5 years, drawing at school

In the school context Lianne had been placed in one of two parallel classes of 30 plus children, each staffed by a teacher and, for part of the day, a classroom assistant. Lianne's teacher was respectful of her right to make private communications. Partly because of her preoccupation with targeting individual children for baseline assessment, she encouraged her to make practical use of a wide range of well organized and accessible materials. These were set out in workshop areas. Lianne had opportunities to internalize and then represent her new understanding in all the workshop areas. In addition, she experienced a range of whole class and group open-ended activities. All were intended to support her in making connections between previous experiences and new learning opportunities across the curriculum.

Making use of the children's attraction to the story form, the teacher sent the class a message, ostensibly from a teddy bear in the stock cupboard. Lianne was drawn to role-play within the 'office' and, in response to this letter, she made use of scissors and tape to send 'messages' in envelopes to her peers. As shown in Figure 7.2, she included drawing and individual letters as part of these narratives, seemingly unaware of the distinction between these

Figure 7.2 Bears and letters

two symbolic forms. Importantly Lianne's teacher modelled the use of drawing alongside verbal, physical and three-dimensional activities. She encouraged the class to represent meanings as a group, valuing all contributions and taking a trial and error approach to decision making. This acted as a stimulus for Lianne to extend the group experience for further personal exploration, without feeling under pressure to achieve a particular outcome.

Lianne's playful, self-directed response to an activity based upon the story book *We're Going on a Bear Hunt* (Oxenbury and Rosen 1992) is shown in Figure 7.3. Her teacher commented:

> I put the table together and we taped bits of paper to the table and we were drawing on the table and we'd made the cave out of something and they were going to get all the objects and we created this map. We told a story using a puppet of the people that were on the bear hunt moving along and she was desperate to get a pen and paper. She chose a large piece of paper from the construction area. She collected a bear and two small world people for her drawing. She drew a bit, then sat up and looked at her drawing before adding to it. She used the bear and people to 'act out' her story. As she drew it she was saying, 'This is the cave, this is all the wishy washy grass, this is all

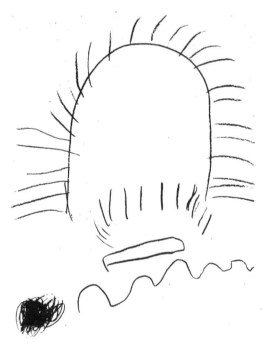

Figure 7.3 Bear hunt

the mud.' She was going, 'squelch, squelch, squelch'. She was saying, 'Whooo this is the snow storm.' She was doing it and her whole body was moving and she was drawing it on paper.

Importantly, the teacher was confident that Lianne's multi-modal meaning making encompassed a range of appropriate learning opportunities. Not only was Lianne's teacher bridging the divide that can often be found between 'play' and 'work' in the reception classroom, but she was unconsciously drawing upon the work of Kress (1997), Dyson (1993a) and Pahl (2002). She actively supported the development of Lianne's multi-modal literacies and encouraged her as a symbol weaver to make meaning through visual, oral and artefactual texts.

At this stage of her life, across both home and school settings, Lianne's engagement in her chosen activities was total, indicating an emotional satisfaction with what she was doing and ensuring she maintained a 'mastery orientation' (Dweck 1986) towards learning.

Lianne 6 years, drawing at home

One year later, Lianne made the difficult transition between the very different contexts of Foundation Stage and Key Stage One within the same school setting. Fortunately, at home she still had the freedom to make meaning in her own way. Lianne's mother commented, 'She's not interested in TV, not at all ... She loves reading. At home I read her favourite stories like *The Little Mermaid*'. Her particular interest in female characters was shown in her role-play which reflected her observation and imitation of everyday rites and rituals of the female role models of mother and teacher. She played 'mums and dads' and 'schools' constantly, always taking the organizing role.

Lianne often brought another same aged friend home to play after school. Alongside their play with 'babies', the two girls used the Barbie-inspired figures of *Mary Poppins*, the *Little Mermaid* and *Anastasia* to re-enact play scripts. These scripts generally featured the 'falling outs' and 'making ups' of friendships, rather than the video-inspired themes that gave the figures their names. The figures within these play episodes generally acted as a prop for talk rather than action.

With access to a plentiful supply of paper and pens, Lianne used drawing, alongside her ongoing play with dolls, as part of her role as mother, or increasingly her role as teacher. Her mother commented:

> She's still drawing before school you know, rushing them off at the last minute ... She copies how her brother does his arms. They're both at it, drawing together ... I have loads of trouble getting her to

do her homework. She's never got time for it . . . She just wants to draw. She doesn't want to do this writing . . . She uses Barbie paper, she has got a little notebook and it's got hearts all over it . . . She's just a doodler, she just has to be doodling.

Alongside registers and replicas of school reward systems, Lianne drew the static, 'lined-up' and labelled figures of family and friends. These drawings reflected her increasing interest in clothing, particularly her fascination with 'high heels' and hairstyles. Her mother reported arguments with Lianne about what was suitable footwear for school and her growing interest in rings, necklaces and earrings. Lianne's use of decorative patterning and the heart motif in particular (Figure 7.4) reflects the prevalence of this iconic motive in

Figure 7.4 Figures on envelope

artefacts marketed for young girls as recognized by Marsh and Millard (2000). Lianne's colourful drawing of a rainbow with sun, clouds and sea (Figure 7.5), completed in the home context, was seen by Lianne's mother to be typical of the drawings that she brought home from school following Lianne's participation in 'wet playtime' drawing sessions with her female peers.

Lianne's patient and gentle older brother, seemingly happy to fit in with his sister's demands, also continued to influence the development of her drawing and writing skills. Her mother actively encouraged Lianne to turn to

Figure 7.5 Rainbow

him for support and she continued to play with and work alongside him as they grew up together, observing and copying the strategies to create particular effects that he modelled.

Lianne, 6 years, drawing at school

In her Year One classroom, the curriculum was separated into distinct subject areas and the Literacy and Numeracy Hours had been introduced. The transition from the reception to the Year One class was particularly stressful for Lianne, given the autonomy and freedom of representation she had experienced across both home and school contexts the previous year. She suddenly lost this freedom as she entered Year One. In common with Holly's experience in her Year One classroom, access to doing and making materials was limited. Resources were focussed on literacy and numeracy activities. Both teachers with parallel Year One classes had decided not to have a role-play area and, given that whole class lessons predominated, it is difficult to see how children would have gained access to it. The classroom physically looked different. Without workshop areas, tables and chairs dominated the room and display areas were designated to literacy, numeracy and ICT priorities. Lianne's mother commented on her daughter's reaction to the changes saying,

'She didn't want to come to school this morning. I asked her why, she just said "cos its boring"'.

The teacher recognized that the constraints of classroom organization and timetabling denied her access to children's behaviours and competences that free play may have promoted. 'If I was never to let them choose some children wouldn't really show me what they were capable of because some of the children, their talents are restricted in the numeracy and literacy because of say their handwriting skills.' In common with Simon and Holly, Lianne had limited opportunities for self-chosen activities. 'Choosing' was allocated a 30 minute block of time following spelling and singing each Friday afternoon.

At this early stage of the new school year, the Year One teacher reported that Lianne was an excitable child who, being very sociable, found it difficult to remain focussed during whole class 'carpet time' when she constantly had to be reminded not to talk. 'I am having to squash her because she is so excitable, so in situations where she is meant to be concentrating on what is going on, she is much more interested in other children.' Lianne's parents, trying hard to support the class teacher, initiated a reward system whereby Lianne received sweets for paying attention and keeping quiet.

The weekly art lesson was interpreted as a teacher directed, whole class activity. This concentration upon a directed approach to drawing, divorced from context, was in stark contrast to the opportunities that had been given for meaning making by Lianne's reception class teacher. In the reception class Lianne's participation in group decision making around two- and three-dimensional activities, stimulated and supported by story and rhyme, led to individual, self-initiated, multi-modal activities. Whereas the pattern of Lianne's day in the reception class had allowed for long periods of uninterrupted activity, her Year One teacher recognized that in order to avoid children having to return to complete an activity one week later, each lesson needed to be complete in itself.

Lianne's Year One teacher collected no evidence of work completed by Lianne during the time allocated for art activity during the period of data collection. Given that across the curriculum activities that did not fit into their prescribed time allocation were left unfinished, there may have been no completed artwork to collect. Figures 7.6 and 7.7 are examples of drawing completed during sessions allocated to other curriculum areas. Children were only allowed to draw after their writing was completed. The content was dominated by an adult agenda and had to be completed under pressure to fit into the timetabled slot.

Lianne's opportunity for playful, self-chosen activities came during playtimes spent with a group of same-age girls. Led by an older girl, she imitated the dance routines and behaviours of favourite pop star performances as seen on video or television. For Lianne this was the best part of the school day.

Figure 7.6 Snacks

Figure 7.7 Cello

In common with Holly's Year One setting, drawing was a wet playtime activity, generally unacknowledged by the teacher, and not recognized or collected as art activity for the research project. However, Lianne's mother acknowledged that, like 6-year-old Holly, Lianne was part of a group of same-aged girls who chose to draw together at school. These group episodes of 'draw and talk' were a key opportunity for Lianne to make her own meaning in the school context, though the drawings also reflected a commonality of both content and style recognized in Dyson's (1986: 389) description of girls' pre-occupation with representing images of 'happy little girls'.

Lianne 7 years, drawing at home

When we returned a year later for the final phase of data collection, it was obvious that the family had lived through a difficult period. The children's father had moved out to live locally with the mother of Lianne's best friend. Her mother felt that Lianne was coping well with the domestic crisis. She admitted that she had been very upset in front of the children. They had tried hard to comfort her.

Figure 7.8 was typical of the kind of drawings Lianne was producing at this time. It reflected a preoccupation with love and friendship, perhaps influenced by her recent experiences of the uncertainty of home relationships, but also a common theme amongst her circle of friends. She began to use writing more than drawing in her representations. At home Lianne continued to 'play out' the school day. Her mother observed and reported to us her copying short stories from reading books, writing letters or completing pages of sums which, as she switched role from pupil to teacher, she then marked.

Unlike her brother, whose representations were strongly influenced by television themes and characters, television was merely a background accompaniment to Lianne's enjoyment of reading fairytale stories about queens and princesses. Having constantly been referred to as 'my little princess' by her mother and father ever since she was little, she identified strongly with this romantic role. Her mother commented, 'She does little books like six pages of A4 and she folds them in half and she does, it's mostly princess stories and things like that ... She thinks she is a princess'.

Her mother noticed that drawing or writing at home had become an increasingly solitary occupation: 'She doesn't want anybody interfering with hers. It's hers'. Her girl friends had become increasingly important to her. When the girls were together at each other's houses they reverted to using drawings in preference to writing, continuing to integrate their worlds of home, school and popular culture through their ongoing dialogue of 'draw and talk' (Figure 7.9).

Figure 7.8 Kiss me

Lianne 7 years, drawing at school

The organization of both the day and the classroom in Lianne's Year Two context replicated the pattern of Year One. There was little time or provision for children to have choices of activity. Only at the end of one teacher

Figure 7.9 Girls drawing outside

directed activity and before another was set, reading a book or working on the computer was allowed for a few minutes. The timetable was dominated by literacy and numeracy with little time for foundation subjects. Lianne's new class teacher recognized the importance of children taking part in decision making and problem solving through paired or group activities. However, the perception of Lianne's mother, as a classroom assistant, was that 'sitting and listening' predominated at Key Stage One.

There was evidence that children's representational activities followed detailed demonstration and modelling by an adult. As in Lianne's Year One context, the only drawings collected by Lianne's Year Two class teacher (Figures 7.10 and 7.11), were completed during taught sessions servicing other curriculum areas. Although the purpose of these labelled diagrams was to gain evidence of Lianne's understanding of scientific concepts, Lianne had extended what was merely an assessment tool into a 'picture' by her addition of, for example, the sun in Figure 7.10. Her teacher acknowledged that there were few opportunities for children to draw pictures and explained, 'At one time and in my teaching it used to be when you'd written it, you drew a picture. My feeling is we've moved away from that a bit . . . we're spending the time on the quality of the writing and the spelling and that there often isn't time to then draw a picture.'

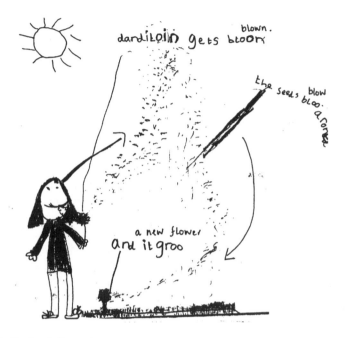

dardilpin gets bloow blown.

the seeds blow arorrw.

a new flower and it groo

Figure 7.10 Seed dispersal

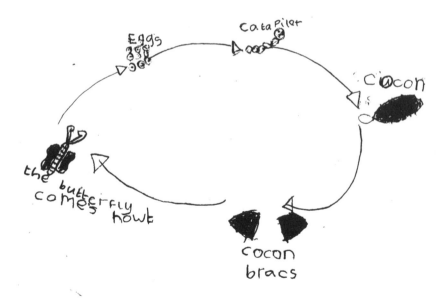

Eggs

Cata piler

cocon

the butterfly comes howt

cocon bracs

Figure 7.11 Lifecycle of butterfly

The content of the QCA art scheme of work, followed this year for the first time by the school, was delivered as a whole class activity within a weekly time slot allocated to art. The class teacher felt that the QCA planned series of lessons were appropriate, but that the 'build up' of art activities and skills had been compromised by having to also follow the school long-term planning. In practice she was required to integrate the Art and Design and Technology Orders within one session of one and a half hours each week. Lianne's class teacher confirmed Matthew's (2001) views about the lack of opportunity given for children to produce art which served their own intentions. Experienced in teaching all infant age groups, she commented, 'There is free choice for art work in the early years, in nursery and reception. Once children leave reception virtually the whole of the art curriculum is part of the teacher taught topic, which in itself comes from the QCA'.

Lianne made the transition from Year One into her Year Two school context comfortably. But her statement 'I like playtime best' and her recognition of wet playtimes as a time when 'you get to choose what you want to play with' drew attention to her longing for self-initiated, playful activity within the prescribed and teacher directed curriculum she experienced.

Summary

Across the three years of the study, strong support was sustained in the home context for Lianne's meaning making through role-play and for her free access to and use of materials and artefacts. Lianne made steady progress through Dyson's (1993a) symbolic continuum. But role-play underpinned her movement into drawing and then into writing as she re-enacted the roles first of mother but then of teacher and pupil. She was lucky that her experiences in the reception classroom enabled her to integrate the worlds of home and school. In contrast, her experiences in her Year One classroom did not allow such connections and consequently did not build on her learning strengths or address her learning needs. Lianne's multi-modal skills were lost to the school context with its requirement of subject separation and its concentration upon 'letteracy'. By the time Lianne entered her Year Two classroom she had learned the restricted requirements of 'being a pupil'. In school she conformed to Key Stage One curriculum expectations and concentrated upon communication through writing. With her girl friends at home she continued to use drawing as a mode of representation and communication.

8 Themes from the seven children's drawings

The stories of Luke's, Simon's, Holly's and Lianne's journeys towards learning to draw and drawing to learn have demonstrated the complexity of the inter-relationships between the home and school influences on their drawing behaviours. There were three more children in our project: Jake, Edward and Donna. Sadly we do not have the space in this book to include full details of their stories too, but we will refer to evidence of their drawings in this chapter.

We had chosen children from a wide range of social backgrounds, except for families from ethnic minorities (see Gregory 1997 and Barratt-Pugh 2000 in the field of early literacy for socio-cultural studies of early literacy in English as a second language contexts). Though each child's family and school story was unique, when we looked across the seven children we found similarities as well as differences.

The specific features of the children's lived experiences at home and school were nested within a wider world of cultural influences:

- the contrasting expectations of what it meant to be male and female modelled by parents, friends, siblings and extended families within their home communities;
- the impact of media and commercial interests on their choice of what and how to represent their understandings and feelings;
- the cultural expectations of what it is to be a pupil and friend in pre-school and infant school settings.

Of course, it is dangerous to generalize from a small sample. But we have gained confidence from our dialogues with the project practitioners and parents, and from the reactions of wider audiences at early years conferences, that what we are saying about the seven children resonated with their wide experience of young children.

Themes from home contexts

A key feature within the home context was the shaping of the children into being a boy or girl. Parents were a powerful influence on the children's emerging gender identities. All of the mothers of our seven children except one worked for at least some of the week. Yet the mothers made themselves available at home either in the background of children's play, including drawing episodes, or as resources, giving support when requested. The girls absorbed the everyday routines and rituals of their mothers, 'playing out' a female nurturing role. They replicated these roles in their domestic play with dolls and small figures. In contrast fathers and older siblings were involved in short episodes of physical play with the children. The girls accommodated their fathers' style of occasional bouts of playfulness, teasing and rough and tumble play. For boys the attraction of their father as male role models was more intense given the short periods they spent together. When their fathers were absent, the boys played out male roles as fighters, adventurers and super heroes, often supported by television imagery.

The children's use of symbol systems was filtered through the distinctive roles taken by mothers and fathers and the cultural messages as to what was appropriate representational behaviour for boys and girls. The girls seemed to progress steadily through Dyson's (1993a) continuum of symbol systems set out in Figure 1.1 in Chapter 1. All the mothers reported that their daughters were content to play out narratives independently for long periods with dolls, soft toys and associated domestic artefacts. Significant people in their real and imagined worlds featured in their drawings as two-dimensional versions of their three-dimensional play activities. They immersed themselves in their mothers' stories about family lives and histories. They drew their female friends. Holly and Lianne's drawings in Figures 6.5 and 7.4 are typical examples.

In contrast the boys demonstrated a preference for three-dimensional elaborate narrative play activities. Their preoccupations reached out to a dynamic world outside domestic contexts. Symbolic representation of people, places and things, unless regularly modelled by a key male figure, was less evident. Instead drawings were likely to feature action, movement and speed, such as Luke's crocodile drawing in Figure 4.2. Action drawings became dynamic extensions of their whole body movement as the drawing tool 'hit' the surface.

Jake, at 4 years old, drew an action drawing representing an elaborate story about magic played with his older sister, Emily. Figure 8.1 shows him standing at a blackboard. His mother vividly recorded the drawing episode in her notes in the scrapbook:

> Emily and Jake were singing about magic spells. Jake was chanting and dancing. He went to the blackboard, picked up some chalk and drew a magic spell boat. He then continued to draw the boat, sea and gangway. He talked all the time, describing what he was drawing. The drawing was energetic and fluid. He used different colours and

Figure 8.1 Magic spells

drew with the tip and the side of the chalk. He made a spell to make lugworms. He chanted 'Abracadabra Lug Worms', striking the board with a red stick of chalk.

Jake and Emily's mother was a part-time teacher and their father a full-time engineer. The children were encouraged by both parents to 'get on with playing'. Mess and exuberance were tolerated. Though the children had a well-resourced playroom, much of their play took place in shared family spaces such as the lounge and kitchen. The easel in Figure 8.1, for example, was within sight of the cooking area. The children were often taken at weekends to places of interest. They were discouraged from watching 'too much' television. There was a culture of doing and talking in the house. Jake's mother reported, 'People always comment on the fact that my children are very verbally expressive. They can paint with words. My husband and I are articulate and spend time talking to the children'. Jake's passion was for three-dimensional representations, particularly construction play. Figure 8.2 shows him working out with Emily how to design and make a Lego cup holder to prevent his mother spilling her coffee in the lounge. As his mother explained: 'Jake is strongly attracted to Dad's activities as an engineer'.

We found that the rules and routines established by mothers impacted on the children's play behaviours. This included tolerance of 'mess', organization

Figure 8.2 Designing a Lego cup holder

of space and time, control over the availability of cultural objects and artefacts, including watching television and videos and, importantly, recognition of children's need to have time free from adult direction. In Jake's case both parents encouraged their children's imaginative interweaving of reality and myth with warmth, good humour and a non-judgemental attitude. Drawing was one of the modes used by the children for representation. But there was no pressure on Jake to move on from his exuberant action drawings towards 'visual realism'. His parents' playful approach to meaning making led him to act unselfconsciously, without fear of criticism. During the second year we visited Jake and his family, his mother recorded the point at which Jake first realized that he could draw 'realistically'. The realization came within the purposeful context of a family game of Pictogram. In this game each player takes turns to draw things which their team has to interpret against the clock. When it came to his turn to draw, Jake drew a recognizable cow with large udders. His team quickly identified the cow. His triumphant achievement evoked much laughter and shared enjoyment. In contrast, parents' attempts to direct drawing activities, such as those initiated by Simon and Luke's parents, could lead to children adopting a 'helpless orientation' (Dweck 1986) towards and rejection of drawing. Sometimes this rejection was temporary; but we suspect that many adults with long-standing anxieties about their ability to draw develop this negative disposition at an early stage of their childhood.

Kress (1997), Pahl, (2001, 2002) and Matthews (2003) argue that it is important for young children to have access to a mixture of drawing materials, toys and everyday objects in order to make multi-modal representations. The mothers controlled opportunities to integrate three- and two-dimensional activity by storage of play resources in the homes. Jake and Emily enjoyed the freedom to access freely a wide range of materials, artefacts and objects.

The child's position within the family also had an impact on affordances and constraints for meaning making. For example, when a child had younger siblings, drawing might be confined to the kitchen table. Parents simply could not risk younger siblings drawing on walls, upholstery and bed linen. Where a child had an older sibling, particularly when they prioritized drawing, the younger child was more likely to have a regular model for drawing behaviour and also paper, pencils and felt tips readily 'to hand'. The influence of such older sibling behaviours on younger children in the family cannot be underestimated.

Each of our seven children experienced changes in family circumstances during the three years of the project. Jake, Luke and Donna moved house. Holly and Donna had new babies in their homes. These significant events, and the strong feelings associated with them, were reflected in their drawings. Holly's powerful representations of her expanding family have already been discussed in Chapter 6. Donna was an only child at the start of the project and, like Holly, a strong character. She attended the same Family Centre as Luke. There she was content to play alone within the sight of her key worker or with a small group of mainly female friends. At home she was encouraged by her equally strong mother to 'stand up for herself'. She happily played alone at home, for example with small figure play, construction and jigsaws, rarely drawing. The television was often on, providing a comforting background. When the family moved to a new home away from busy roads Donna was allowed to play out with older girls. When she settled into school she could take or leave most classroom activities. But she became totally absorbed in playground activities. She sought out her older girl companions to join in animated talk of jewellery, make-up, pop stars and boyfriends. The arrival of her new baby sister, Elizabeth, precipitated an unusual spate of drawing at home. The drawings were done in close physical proximity to her mother and the new baby. Her mother told us, 'When I came home from hospital, I was only gone six hours and she was getting really emotional . . . She did a lot [of drawings] when I'd had Elizabeth. She wouldn't leave my side so they were all on the kitchen wall, all her drawings'. Figure 8.3 is one of these: a drawing of a doll Donna made for her new sister.

As we have seen with Donna, it is not only family, but friends, who influence what young children value and chose to represent. In Edward's home environment, he was constantly competing for his father's attention with his very able, 11-year-old sister. There were regular arguments between the children

Figure 8.3   Doll for baby sister

and Edward was often chided as the protagonist. Reconciling differences by confrontation hovered in the atmosphere. Edward appeared not to value his mother as a play partner. His father worked long hours, but he was Edward's preferred play partner – usually involving a three-dimensional construction kit. Father and son watched wrestling on TV together. The toys were confined to the children's bedrooms, so there were no opportunities for the kind of free-flowing play around the house Jake and his sister enjoyed. Access to paper and pencil was confined to homework. Perhaps because his play opportunities were constrained indoors, Edward preferred to be outside with his bike. His parents were constantly anxious that he would get involved with the misbehaviour of older boys in the street. He showed little interest in drawing until a slightly older boy with a passion for drawing armies joined the street gang. Then he responded enthusiastically as the older boy modelled action narratives in drawings involving power and conquest, explosions and battles, and the technical machinery involved in killing and destruction. Figure 8.4, his drawing of a tank, is an example. His mother told us, 'He's got a new friend who's moved in up the road who likes armies, wears all these camouflage clothes and shows Edward all his military things. Now Edward wants to draw army pictures all the time ... My brother used to be in the Marines and in the Army Artillery Corps and he asked, "Can I ring him up and see if he's got any old books on the army?"'

Figure 8.4 Army tank

The affordances and constraints in the seven children's lived experiences, informal learning opportunities and emerging identities at home were mirrored in the drawings pasted into their scrapbooks by parents. As we identified themes emerging from pre-school and infant school contexts, we found patterns of affordances and constraints to their meaning making as they adopted identities as pupils.

Themes from Foundation Stage contexts

As the children made the transition from home to pre-school contexts, the girls found a continuity of experience as they entered the female dominated world of early childhood education and care. They opted to play with the dolls and artefacts familiar at home in the home corners and with tabletop toys alongside adults. The boys, anxious to maintain their sense of identity as male and dissociate themselves from the domestic female world at home (Bailey 1993), appeared less confident. Sometimes they latched on to nurturing girls as substitute 'mothers' until they established friendships with boys. Then they opted for boisterous physical play involving wheeled vehicles and adventures, outdoors when allowed, and, when not, in construction play spread across the floor.

The female practitioners who dominated the daily worlds of Foundation Stage settings talked about drawing in child development terms. 'We talk about stages and what they're going on to.' In the Family Centre attended by Luke and Donna a key worker described progression in drawing as from, 'to and fro scribbles or a line or two, [which] then progress to circular scribbling, then [to] marks with some intent such as a person, body, arms and legs, and then [to having] some detail on it'. Each child's progress was recorded on a developmental checklist. Because of the emphasis in day-care culture of sitting alongside and paying individualized attention to children, particularly in the afternoon 'key worker' sessions, practitioners were able to tune into the children's preoccupations. For example, Luke's key worker was aware of his interest in media imagery and crocodiles. However, day-care staff felt under pressure to coach children towards the 'next stage' of drawing. An example was given in Chapter 4 at Figure 4.3 of Luke being encouraged to draw his Mam. The nursery officers were ambivalent about how much to direct children. One told us, 'Sometimes I am not quite sure what I should say. But if they're drawing a picture of a car, I'll say, "That's the roof and these are the wheels", and I'll say, "Let's see if we can find a book with a picture of a car". We'll talk about it. What we can transfer to the drawing.'

Traditionally in day-care settings drawing had been a relaxing activity, freely chosen at a mark making table. As we pointed out in Chapter 2, from 2000 the Foundation Stage Curriculum must be delivered to 3- and 4-year-olds in all UK settings where an 'educational component' is funded. The manager in Luke and Donna's Family Centre told us that now her staff felt under pressure to focus on progression from drawing to emergent literacy. The pressure was pushing staff to use worksheets to promote pencil control and knowledge of shapes. The manager said:

> When we hear the phrase mark-making, it doesn't matter how many times you go through it with them, they think writing. It's there in the back of their mind all the time. That's not to say if child did a row of circles they wouldn't be impressed by that, but only because it's starting to look like letters. They feel that's what they ought to be ... they know the benefits, they know the therapy that children get from expressing, from experiencing. But their own vulnerability will always lead them to think in terms of writing, particularly if they're talking to knowledgeable people.

In this pre-school climate the girls' capacity to draw people met with approval. In contrast the boys' action drawings were not valued. The boys rejected the practitioners' well meaning attempts to force figure drawing upon them. They continued to represent in three-dimensional modes. Their activities in small figure play and the construction area were validated by adult and male peer approval. In contrast there was often hostility from the mainly female practitioner workforce towards boys' exploration in role-play and drawings of the powerful issues of good and evil which underpinned their preoccupation with superheroes (Davies 1989; Holland 2000; MacNaughton 2000).

In nursery and reception classes in primary schools mark making tables were often set up as role-play areas such as 'offices', travel agents or paper shops. Though in theory the children were free to pursue a personal agenda, the role-play framework set up by the adults shaped drawings. Drawing was also used as an adult directed activity to service half-termly topics 'to record pictorially the things they've learnt and to reinforce new concepts'. Channelled within a teacher chosen theme, the children's drawings lacked spontaneity. Their voices were submerged beneath the over-riding imperative of a teacher interpreted curriculum. The discourse of Simon's, Holly's and Jake's nursery teacher reflected a concern with developing skills: 'fine motor control, learning new techniques ... beginning to hold the pencil and realising there are different ways of making marks with different materials, selecting the correct materials for the purpose ... the right paper ... so doing a plan in the construction area or the brick corner they might use squared paper'. Practitioners adopted a role as facilitators of children's drawing development, and were ambivalent about feedback, 'We would never say what's wrong or right, but we might pose the questions, "What do you think if ...? Have you thought about...?"'

There was little recognition of the need for children to move across domains of provision in the pre-school settings. 'Workshop' areas allowed children to focus upon one activity, but they worked against the 'joined-upness' discouraging the kind of transformative meaning making described by Pahl (1999). In contrast, Lianne's reception teacher was unusual in offering the children in her classroom opportunities to mix modes of meaning making. Lianne's lively drawings from this context are shown in Figures 7.2 and 7.3. In addition to an office and role-play area, Lianne's teacher stocked a large drawer from which the children could freely access string, cardboard, fabrics, etc. She ensured that the children had access to connecting and drawing tools: scissors, tape, pens and pencils. She acknowledged the need for 'mess'. In her planned teacher initiated focus sessions she supported children in integrating home and school knowledge and ensured that in the midst of curriculum requirements their 'voices' were heard. She listened carefully to the narratives accompanying the children's 'meaning makings' and was knowledgeable about their preoccupations.

She saw the role of adults as to instruct as well as facilitate children's progress in drawing. This quotation expresses her uncertainty about the pedagogy of drawing. It also shows how even this enlightened reception class teacher perceived writing as a higher status mode of representation:

When we did self-portraits, I drew my face on the board first and we touched our eyebrows and our noses. But I don't mind if they are less accurate in their drawing than in their writing. If a child brought a drawing to me and it was a huge potato head and a small body, I wouldn't correct them. I'd say, 'Oh, that's lovely. You've got a Smiley Face for that. That's great.' But if they brought something to me and they'd written their name and there's a capital letter in the middle, I'd know I didn't want that, and I'd use the opportunity to sort it out … I've stopped myself saying, 'Dogs don't have five legs, do they?' Because if that child's representation of a dog has six legs, that's them expressing themselves. It's artistic licence.

Themes from Key Stage One contexts

As described in Chapter 1, once the children began 'formal education' within the subject-based framework of the National Curriculum their learning environment changed, sometimes with dramatic effects on their dispositions to learn. Within Key Stage One contexts the political beliefs and values which underpin government policy and legislation at macro level impacted upon the culture of schooling. These factors included messages given by Ofsted inspections, local authority training, headteacher priorities, parental pressures and the media to practitioners. Practitioners' approaches to drawing, art and creative activities were interpreted through experiences of initial teacher training, understanding of child development and their own personal experiences of art education.

As the National Curriculum and Literacy and Numeracy Strategies rolled into primary schools, teachers who had been trained to work an 'integrated day' in which children worked in groups on a variety of tasks across the curriculum, radically re-orientated their style of pedagogy. One of the teachers in the project admitted that she had learned about whole class teaching from a student teacher. She found it 'easier to manage … easier to track that the children had covered everything … demanding children with behaviour problems were much easier to keep settled'. The down side she admitted was having 'very little time for individuals now. I don't get the chance to talk to the children like I used to'. Another teacher admitted that whole class teaching suited 80 per cent of her class. Twenty per cent 'mostly the boys, mostly the immature children, the middle to low ability children' found it hard 'to sit still on a chair for so long'. She felt they missed out on one to one interactions which had in the past kept them motivated.

Literacy and numeracy dominated the morning timetable. Art and other foundation subjects were allocated 45 minute afternoon slots each week or fortnight. The art areas remained as totems in most classrooms used for storage of materials. Whole class art lessons in beautifully carpeted classrooms constrained the children by the need not to spill paint or glue. Lessons consisted of one-off tasks, often within a sequence in QCA schemes of work, as described in Chapter 1. As one teacher put it, 'We do collective art, like collective worship. We do art on a Tuesday afternoon'. Within a tight structure of a whole class introduction and prescribed art activity, this teacher was still concerned to offer the children opportunities for personal expression.

> That is the opportunity for their individuality to come out. We don't say that you have to go away and do it exactly as we say but, 'Now we would like you to go away and have a go at something like that'. Then you get the ones that really, really love it and they take ages over it and they really express . . . and the ones who just whip it off in ten seconds flat.

One of our teachers, an art coordinator, talked to us about the pedagogy of art teaching at Key Stage One:

> I think a lot of teachers are a bit frightened of saying to a child, 'that could be improved'. I think we were encouraged a few years ago to say about all art work, 'Oh, isn't that wonderful!' But now we tend to look at what the task was and how we could improve it. We might be looking at the size of it or the shape of it, how it has got texture, how you might shade it, how they could use different media to make it any better. But I like to try and ask the children what they think of it and ask them if they think they can improve it as well.

Drawing was also used as a 'time-filler' following the completion of teacher directed activities. These five to ten minute slots gave little opportunity for a child to develop a drawing. In contrast with Foundation Stage contexts where there was a reasonable balance of child chosen and teacher directed activity, time for child chosen activity was often restricted to half an hour on a Friday afternoon, sometimes called 'Golden Time'. A Year One teacher described her children's reaction to being offered drawing during Golden Time. 'As soon as I say they can choose they are like bees in a workhouse. They know just what they want to do. They love it. If I gave them an hour they'd keep busy the whole hour and they do some really lovely stuff.'

As children moved from the reception class into Year One, they tried to make sense of the continuities and discontinuities between Foundation Stage and Key Stage One provision. For Simon, a child who relied on his mother or sister to initiate activities and whose pre-school background had encultured him into seat-based activities with pencil and paper, the move was reassuring. But for boys whose primary mode of meaning making was still three-dimensional play, the transfer to Year One required them to bypass drawing. Practitioners failed to recognize the mediating role of drawing between their mastery of three-dimensional activity and their capacity to cope with the abstract symbolism of writing. Jake was lucky enough to have a mother who understood the 'school world' of letteracy. She was concerned about a clash between his quicksilver ways and physical exuberance, and school culture. In the summer before he started formal school, she coached him into mastery of writing his name and numbers up to ten. She explained that if he completed these tasks quickly, he would be allowed to go and play with construction toys. So it proved to be. Jake was perceived by his Year One teacher to be 'school ready' and therefore, ironically, allowed to access more play-based activities. He made a comfortable transition to being a pupil at Key Stage One.

Children who were experienced, autonomous decision makers across home and pre-school found the transition to Key Stage One traumatic. Lianne's mother spoke of her daughter's shock at the transfer, her tears in not wanting to go to school and her boredom with a classroom where there was 'nothing to do'. Lianne's classroom environment prioritized the symbol systems of letters and numbers rather than visual images. The forms of meaning making available to her were suddenly narrowed. She had the confidence and home support to adjust to the demands of this formal learning context. Her trauma was not communicated to her teacher. As the teacher quoted above told us, practitioners' access to children as individuals was restricted by the organizational structures of whole class teaching. But practitioners found it hard to ignore the increase in aggressive behaviour as children, particularly boys, attempted to gain power and control on the playground during playtimes. They failed to make connections between children's aggressive behaviour and their loss of autonomy within an imposed and prescribed curriculum and rigid classroom organization.

Out in the playground we observed the children's fascination with and imitation of the gendered activities of their older peers. Boys were attracted as spectators to older boys' football games. They grouped together under the leadership of a dominant male to re-enact in physical play the power struggles of good and evil of superhero narratives. During wet playtimes they played out superhero themes in small figure and construction play. If construction materials were not available, drawing became a second choice occupation, recognized by both boys and girls as a gender-neutral activity. Pairs or small groups of boys came together to develop a common interest. Their drawings often reflected television and Play Station imagery and their continuing fascination with movement and power: football, robots and army battles. The female practitioners in our project collected little evidence of wet playtime drawings. They did not reflect a 'school' agenda.

The girls' playground activities included watching and replaying the actions of older girls: songs and dance routines of favourite pop groups and exchanges of information about fashions in hairstyles, jewellery and clothing. As a wet playtime option large groups of girls congregated around tables to draw and talk. These 'drawing clubs' offered girls a site to explore being female but also, as recognized by Dyson (1993b), an opportunity to integrate the culture from home communities with their transformed version of the 'official' world of school. The content of their drawings reflected not only the growing influence of the decorative cartoon heroines of video imagery and their fascination with hair length and shoe height, but also their replaying of the teacher's role through, for example, the completing of registers and ticking of sums.

The children's transition from Year One into Year Two was smoother. By now they had learned how to be pupils. Their expectations of a mainly seat-based, writing dominated curriculum, strongly directed by the teacher were confirmed by their experiences. Teachers did not make the connection between drawing skills taught in art lessons and their expectations of children of drawing to illustrate knowledge across other curriculum subjects. Children developed a 'catch all' drawing style to illustrate their work in science, geography, history and English. Teachers did not think of drawing genres in the way they understood that writing fitted into genres. So for example Simon, a consummate drawer, was given little help in making the transition to a technical drawing genre in his attempts to draw a design for a puppet in Figure 5.12.

Outside the school box the children continued to develop their own use of drawing for personal meaning making and to communicate with others. There was little continuity in their approaches to drawing in the different contexts of home and school. As we move into a world where 'reading' texts depends on visual literacy as much as, or maybe even more than, decoding written texts, it is worth reminding ourselves of the control these young children were exhibiting at home over multi-modal representations. These impressive capabilities were being lost in the culture of classrooms. Their teachers were simply not trained to understand how children learn through two- and three- dimensional representations. They were not able to hear the 'voices' embedded in the drawings of these seven young children. It is to the implications of these findings that we turn for the final chapter of the book.

9   Implications

We were privileged to be given access over a three-year period to the home and school worlds of Luke, Simon, Holly, Lianne, Jake, Donna and Edward. Born on the cusp of the new millennium the seven children are representatives of versions of childhood at the macro level of national, regional and local politics and policy in services for young children and their families in England. They are also representatives of how childhood is understood and shaped at the micro levels of their community, family and classroom contexts at this socio-cultural-historical period.

We understood the importance of the messages at macro and micro levels the children received from significant others – media presenters, teachers, parents, siblings and friends. These messages shaped their emerging identities as boys and girls, sons and daughters, friends and learners. Cultural mores modelled by significant others in their lives shaped how the children represented and communicated their understanding of the world around them. Drawing was one of the modes of meaning making available to them. By tuning into their drawings we were able to listen to the seven children's voices. We were also able to use evidence of their drawings, and other images of their representations through three-dimensional models and play with small figures and objects, to engage their parents and practitioners in dialogues about young children's meaning making. We hope that in writing this book the dialogue has been extended to you as readers.

In this final chapter we will pull together implications of our research for parents, practitioners and policy makers, in fact for all of us with responsibility for or an interest in the future well being, learning and fulfilment of young children.

Implications for children's development

There is a growing interest in the power of narrative, not just as a precursor to learning how to read, but as a powerful tool for promoting children's cognitive development. In studies of how young children learn education-based measures of progress have been dominated by items based on attainments in literacy and numeracy. We have relied heavily on these narrowly conceived items of achievement to demonstrate the effectiveness of pre-school education. We have not opened our minds to the interplay between narratives expressed in the modes of speech, play, drawing and symbolic representations in young children's development. Yet Egan (1988) argued many years ago that the story form was a rich, universal, cultural resource for making sense of the world and our experiences within it. The point about narratives is that they can encapsulate cognitive, affective and aesthetic aspects of understanding. So for young children they offer powerful tools for expressing complex ideas. Making drawings gives young children opportunities to represent intricate personal narratives and use them to communicate with significant others in their lives. As Malchiodi (1998) argues, drawing offers a window into children's preoccupations, passions, problems and possibilities. Currently, many adults' potential for hearing and responding to these narratives is limited by their lack of understanding of the power and meaning of children's drawings. We hope that this book will play its part in raising awareness of the importance of drawing in young children's development.

Children also create elaborate narratives in their play with three-dimensional materials – small figures and objects. At home play is often alone or in parallel with siblings. Later pre-school settings offer them opportunities for play in pairs or small groups. Their play story lines are fluid and fanciful yet retain a basic structure of characters, actions and plot. The impact of media imagery on children's three-dimensional play is potent. Children immerse themselves in the powerful images of television and computer game productions. In what Csiksentmihalyi (1979) termed a 'flow' state, they explore in play the abstract concepts of good and evil, power and vulnerability, love and hate, death and destruction embedded in the canon of popular culture just as previous generations used myths, legends and fairy tales. These explorations are strongly gendered: boys focussing on imagery based on fast moving objects, action involving conflict and its resolution and physical exuberance, and girls on imagery based on human relationships, love and loss and physical beauty. We are only just beginning to understand how important such play opportunities are in helping children to come to terms – both conceptually and affectively – with powerful and emotionally charged concepts. At a conceptual level they are learning how to order, explain and represent abstract ideas. At an affective level they are learning how to come to terms with strong emotions and deploy appropriate behaviours in responding to them. Set lessons for 5-year-olds on citizenship are unlikely to have such a strong impact on our young children's social and emotional development.

Young children's spontaneous representations are multi-modal (see references to Kress's seminal work in Chapter 1). Kress (1997) recorded episodes of his young children using a range of resources around the house – discarded greeting cards, household objects, toys, found materials such as egg-boxes and cereal packets – in a rich mêlée of meaning making. He noticed that his children used cut outs of their own drawings and pasted them onto other two-dimensional images. These cut outs appeared to bridge a gap between two- and three-dimensional representations for his children. It was clear to us from our observations of the seven project children that contexts which 'allowed' them to operate with this kind of fluidity to transform things, objects and drawing in free play were empowering for them. Their quixotic use of materials is reflected in rapid shifts from one mode of representing play themes to another: chanting, gesturing, dancing, making, drawing, moving. Paley (1986b) paints a vivid picture of such play:

> The children sounded like groups of actors, rehearsing spontaneous skits on a moving stage, blending into one another's plots, carrying on philosophical debates while borrowing freely from the fragments of dialogue that floated by. Themes from fairy tales and television cartoons mixed easily with social commentary and private fantasies, so that what to me sounded random and erratic formed a familiar and comfortable world for the children.
>
> (Paley 1986b: 125)

Children also absorb information about the symbol systems used by their parents and siblings in everyday communication and modelled in the media – both static images from street advertisements and shop signs and moving images from television and computer screens. Dyson (1993a) provided us with a useful way of conceptualizing how drawing fitted into the children's journeys towards using the symbol systems modelled to them within the cultural contexts in which they learn to make meanings (see Figure 1.1 in Chapter 1). Dyson's model highlights the inter-relationship of gesture, speech, play, drawing and writing in young children's communication. The pattern of development towards symbolic representation is delineated as both sequential and cumulative. She sees collaborative, playful talk between children or between adults playing with children as supporting the evolution of drawing and later writing. But adults must be able to 'tune into' young children's drawing behaviours and listen to the meanings of their early 'action' drawings, rather than push them into the 'status' symbolic representation of visual realism too soon. Above all children should not be made to feel that drawing is only a 'temporary' holding form of symbolic representation leading to mastery of the 'higher level' ability to form letters and numbers. The importance of drawing in its own right should be acknowledged and conveyed to children.

Finally, children's sense of aesthetics is partly culturally acquired by immersion in popular culture – Disney cartoons, videos from children's television series, advertising, greeting cards, sport and fashion. As we have argued in Chapter 8, these aesthetic preferences are often gender specific and media driven. Yet each child develops its own personal style of drawing.

If you are a parent or practitioner with young children, you will be able to recognize which drawings were done by particular children. Sometimes young children's sense of design – where to place marks on a piece of paper – seems bound up with their physical capabilities, as so eloquently observed by Matthews (1999) (see Chapter 2 for an account of his research). But it is clear that they also develop strongly personal preferences for what they want to draw and how they want to draw it. It is important that adults respect the children's growing sense of their own aesthetic sensitivities, rather than coaxing them into a formulaic way of drawing. This is not to argue against adults and siblings supporting children's drawing development, but we will turn to the 'pedagogy of drawing' later in the chapter.

Implications for home contexts

We are all vulnerable to negative feedback from those who have 'power' over us: parents, teachers, bosses, partners. But young children are at the beginning of forging their identities as competent or incompetent learners, popular or unpopular friends, boys or girls. These general positive and negative constructs of self subdivide into more specific features of self-esteem, including one who can draw and one who cannot draw. Parents who value and work with young children's preferred learning and representational modes are more likely to support their children in developing a positive/mastery orientation towards self as learner in general. They can also have a positive impact on children's sense of self as artist.

So what can parents contribute to encouraging children to feel good about being and becoming someone who can draw and enjoys drawing? In the first instance, they can provide an ethos at home where children are encouraged to play freely – sometimes alone on self-chosen activities and sometimes alongside or with parents and siblings. They can also ensure that children have easy access to a wide range of materials for meaning making – materials for drawing, pasting, cutting, painting, fixing, modelling and so on – and that these can be combined when the child wants to do so with play with small figures, bricks, Lego, toys or, as often may be the case, in front of the television. All this openness requires a tolerance of mess whilst children are involved in play episodes. It goes without saying that the children also need guidance in behaving respectfully towards 'adult' spaces, clearing away the mess when their games are over to leave adults time and space for relaxation.

The second contribution parents can make is in responding actively to their children's drawings. This involves tuning sensitively into their drawing as they do them; not breathing down their necks and incessantly asking questions such as, 'What is it?' but rather entering a dialogue with them.

In fact, drawing alongside children can provide great opportunities for chattering about what is preoccupying both generations. It allows adults and children to engage together in what Schaffer (1992) called 'joint involvement episodes'. The focus of drawing might be on a shared experience of a video story, or of a visit to the shops, or shared dreams about a future holiday or Christmas day. It is the way children of different ages quite naturally draw together and learn from each other. This modelling of drawing behaviours seems a fundamentally different approach than an adult drawing something for a child to 'copy'. Sometimes 'tuning in' means tiptoeing away. It is inappropriate to interrupt a child who is totally absorbed in drawing, often accompanied by verbalizing their thinking out loud. But later it may feel right for a parent to talk with the child about the completed drawing. They are likely to gain rich insights into their children's imaginations and preoccupations.

But what do you do when children reach that distressing stage of being frustrated by their inability to do representational drawings, of not being able to make things look like things? If parents have tuned into their children's drawing behaviours from the earliest episodes of mark making, their support through this frustration should be only an extension of a respectful, reciprocal pattern of adult/child interactions already well established. As Matthews argued, 'Babies need an adult companion sharing in the representational adventure in which meanings are given to sounds, actions and images' (Matthews 1994: 123). Parents can help by making suggestions, modelling strategies, looking at images in books or photographs or guiding their children to look at familiar objects carefully, talking them through the outline shape and salient features of what it is they are trying to represent. For Matthews the primary role of parents is to try to understand what the child is trying to do in their drawing, to talk with them about their drawings with respect, and to thus develop a shared family discourse and understanding about drawing. This kind of common sense approach parallels what we know about effective parental strategies for supporting young children's learning about literacy in home contexts (see Weinberger 1996; Barratt-Pugh 2000).

Implications for educational contexts

What are the implications for practitioners' approaches to promoting young children's learning to draw and drawing to learn? We need to think about the nature of the curriculum offered to children, how curriculum activities are experienced by them and what role significant adults in the complementary contexts of home and school play in children's drawing development.

With reference to the curriculum, we need to rethink how what we do with young children reflects the kinds of communication systems and processes that will form the basis of their life styles in the next half century. In England the Foundation Stage curriculum includes 'communication' within language and literacy learning. However, we need exemplars in the guidelines for the implementation of the curriculum which give a sense of the multi-modality of young children's communication. Their fluidity of thinking and acting are already reflected in everyday communication systems in the real world. Within the next half century such changes will escalate into mainstream communication systems as they become increasingly electronic- and global-based.

We also need a radical review of the content of initial teacher training and senior practitioner training programmes. Currently there is an over-emphasis on the teaching of reading and writing, with little attention paid to multi-modal aspects of communication. The current limitations on the scope of curriculum coverage in initial teacher training programmes is directly related to the constraints imposed on providers by narrowly conceived standards designed by the Teacher Training Authority (TTA) and policed by Ofsted. Newly designed Foundation Degrees for senior practitioners have more scope for covering broad aspects of children's learning. A further source of broadly based training is the Childhood Studies Degree now taught in many UK universities. But we lack trainers who are themselves knowledgeable about multi-modality. Many of our potential tutors were trained under the constraints of the TTA standards dominated by preparation to deliver the subject-led framework of the National Curriculum.

We also need clarification about the pedagogy of play. There are token sessions on the centrality of play in training programmes. But we have years of research evidence that shows practitioners are unable to translate their theoretical grasp on the importance of play in young children's learning into their practice in early years settings (see Sylva *et al.* 1980; Meadows and Cashdan 1983; Bennett *et al.* 1997; Siraj-Blatchford 2004). As Bruner argued, 'Play provides an excellent opportunity to try combinations of behaviour that wouldn't be tried under functional pressure' (Bruner 1976: 82). We know that play offers children opportunities to learn within highly motivating and challenging contexts. Yet we still find it hard to articulate and act upon this knowledge. We need high quality research to be funded where practitioners and academics explore together and articulate the complexities of promoting effective learning through play. We need practitioners who understand how to resource, structure, scaffold and discriminate between opportunities children need for both self-initiated and adult led play. We need to learn how to promote the kind of 'flow' state imaginative play described by Paley (1986b), Pahl (1999) and Broadhead (2004) and which is such an impressive feature of the Reggio Emilia approach to early childhood education (Edwards *et al.* 1993).

Sadly, that kind of creative and highly imaginative play, which was a strong feature of our nursery schools' practice in the UK, has been eroded with their demise. At policy level 'play', like 'scribbling', became demonized within the discourse of the standards agenda over the last wearisome two decades. Yet the Foundation Stage guidance now states firmly that play should feature centrally in early years settings.

> Well-planned play, both indoors and outdoors, is a key way in which young children learn with enjoyment and challenge ... Through play, in a secure environment with effective adult support children can: explore, develop and represent learning experiences that help them make sense of the world; practise and build up ideas, concepts and skills; learn how to control impulses and understand the need for rules; be alone, be alongside others or cooperate as they talk or rehearse their feelings; take risks and make mistakes; think creatively and imaginatively; communicate with others as they investigate or solve problems; express fears or relive anxious experiences in controlled and safe situations.
>
> (QCA/DfEE 2000b: 25)

We need to ensure that we can turn that guidance into high quality practice. It is also important that practitioners learn how to respond positively to the preferred play activities of boys, using the kinds of strategies outlined by Holland (2000), MacNaughton (2000) and Jones (2001) so that boys are not alienated from school learning at the crucial period of their emergent identity as pupils. Skelton and Hall (2001) have collated a comprehensive review of literature on sex role stereotyping in early childhood settings to support practitioners in confronting the problems.

A wide range of practitioners with diverse patterns of training are charged with delivering the content of the Foundation Stage Curriculum (Moyles *et al.* 2002). Many 3- and 4-year-olds are educated outside schools. They attend voluntary sector pre-school playgroups or maintained sector Family (day-care) Centres or independent nursery day-care classes. With much to pre-occupy them in getting to grips with delivering the six areas of learning (see Chapter 1 for details), practitioners remain confused about how drawing fits into the Foundation Stage curriculum framework. The Foundation Stage Guidance (QCA/DfEE 2000b) provides little support. Under the heading of creative development the term 'mark making' is used. But in the section on language and literacy 'drawing' is referenced as a 'stepping stone' preceding mark making and writing.

Many practitioners remain fixed in the mindset of developmental stage theory approaches to drawing or, as we have seen in Chapter 8, in the expectation that drawing must lead directly into early writing. There are few experienced trainers in the field of art education able to help practitioners understand the pedagogy of drawing in supporting generalist approaches to training early years practitioners. Art specialists have been culled as the teacher and nursery officer training curriculum requirements for preparation to teach foundations subjects of the National Curriculum narrowed. Art advisers within Local Authorities have been re-deployed as inspectors of general standards. There are some good quality resources promoted by the Campaign for Drawing (www.drawingpower.org.uk), but their excellent website reaches a small proportion of practitioners. So a campaign to empower practitioners with an understanding of how drawing can support and extend young children's learning in pre-school settings is going to be challenging.

Many of our 3- and 4-year-olds are in nursery or reception classes in primary schools in England. Local Authorities are encouraging headteachers to combine nursery and reception classes into Early Years Units for children from 3 to 5 years old. The logistics of organizing and stimulating the learning of part-time and full-time pupils between the ages of 3 and 5 in Early Years Units are challenging. We still seem unsure about how best to deploy the expertise of the teams of workers (teachers, nursery officers, classroom support assistants, voluntary and student helpers). Nor do we seem clear about what forms of organization and pedagogy best fit particular groups of children for specific learning intentions across the six areas of experience of the Foundation Stage. Currently the Qualifications and Curriculum Authority (QCA 2003) is working on materials to support practitioners in promoting creativity across the six areas of experience in early years settings. Following the NACCCE report they have already produced guidance for Key Stage One practitioners as referenced in Chapter 1 (see *Creativity: Find It, Promote It* at www.qca.org.uk).

What are the implications of what we have learned from the project for when children make the transition from the Foundation Stage to the statutory Key Stage One curriculum at the age of 5? We need to remember that when our 5-year-olds make the transition to Key Stage One in England, in many European, Australian and New Zealand contexts 5-year-olds are still categorized as kindergarten children. The argument that we should be introducing 5-year-olds to a less rigid timetable and more integrated curriculum is beginning to be won within the framework of the 'too formal too soon' debates referenced in Chapter 1. In particular, evidence from the project substantiates the growing concern about boys' disaffection with school learning when they are pushed too quickly into writing and recording numerals. At 5 boys' hand/eye skills and physical coordination are less well advanced than those of girls of the same age. But still the daily literacy and numeracy hours, with tasks associated with formal recorded writing and number work, dominate the timetables of most Year One children in English primary schools. The 'back to basics' underpinning of the Standard Assessment Tasks targets in primary schools forces teachers to narrow their literacy curriculum. The Key Stage One curriculum does not reflect the wide range of literacies children and their families are encountering in the real world. The discrete subject basis of the formal literacy and numeracy hours and the subject-based National Curriculum timetables for 5- to 7-year-olds do not encourage children to translate the range of multi-modal representations or screen-based experimentation that many are utilizing at home into school-based learning strategies.

At Key Stage One art is defined as a body of knowledge to be transmitted to children. Drawing activities within timetabled art lessons are driven by fine art constructs of observational and representational drawing. Skill in art is assumed to be the ability 'to make pictures of how three-dimensional objects appear as if seen from a fixed point in space' (Matthews 2003: 34). The contribution of children to the process of creating meanings in drawing is scarcely acknowledged. Drawing across the curriculum is untutored, so that even within technology sessions, teachers rarely explain how specialized this genre of drawing is, nor do they spend time teaching children how to think, plan and represent in designerly ways (Anning 1997b). Time for freely chosen drawing is limited to wet playtimes. Less and less attention is paid to training Key Stage One teachers to teach art. As our quotations from practitioners in Chapter 8 demonstrated, they are unsure about how or when to intervene to support children's progression in drawing. This uncertainty about the pedagogy of drawing is just one aspect of a general confusion over appropriate pedagogy for promoting the learning of young children (Siraj-Blatchford *et al.* 2002).

Conclusion

Our young children deserve better than this. We need to re-affirm the centrality of creativity in their thinking and learning. We need to recognize that multi-modality is core to their preferred ways of representing and communicating their growing understanding of the world and their roles as active members of communities. We need parents to gain confidence in their own intuitive and learned skills in becoming their children's first and most important teachers – including their capabilities in drawing. We need practitioners who have the courage to press for a radical revision of the curriculum for young children and argue for the importance of drawing within that curriculum. We need politicians and policy makers who have the strength and humility to admit where they got some things wrong in early childhood education. We need researchers who can explore and explain the pedagogy of play and creativity and the role of drawing within playful, creative and learning behaviours. We need a society that can listen to children and recognize that perhaps their drawings may tell us much more about childhood than we ever imagined.

References

Abbs, P. (1987) Towards a coherent art aesthetic, in P. Abbs (ed.) *The Arts in Education*. Lewes: The Falmer Press.

Ahlberg, J. and Ahlberg, A. (1983) *Funny Bones*: Scholastic.

Alderson, P. (1995) *Listening to Children: Ethics and Social Research*. Ilford: Barnardos.

Anning, A. (1995) Art, in A. Anning (ed.) *A National Curriculum for the Early Years*. Buckingham: Open University Press.

Anning, A. (1997a) *The First Years at School*, 2nd edn. Buckingham: Open University Press.

Anning, A. (1997b) Drawing out ideas; graphicacy and young children, *International Journal of Technology and Design Education*, 7(3): 219–39.

Anning, A. and Edwards, A. (1999) *Promoting Children's Learning from Birth to Five*. Buckingham: Open University Press.

Arnheim, R. (1969) *Visual Thinking*. London: Faber and Faber.

Athey, C. (1990) *Extending Thought in Young Children*. London: Paul Chapman Publishing.

Bailey, K.R. (1993) *The Girls Are the Ones with Pointy Nails*. Ontario: The Althouse Press.

Barratt-Pugh, C. (2000) The socio-cultural context of literacy learning, in C. Barratt-Pugh and M. Rohl (eds) *Literacy Learning in the Early Years*. Buckingham: Open University Press.

Bennett, N., Wood, E. and Roger, S. (1997) *Teaching Through Play: Teachers' Thinking and Classroom Practice*. Buckingham: Open University Press.

Bissex, G.L. (1980) *GNYS AT WRK: A Child Learns to Read and Write*. Cambridge, MA: Harvard University Press.

Blake, D. (1988) Roger's world. Unpublished document, University of Massachussets, Boston.

Broadhead, P. (2004) *Early Years Play and Learning: Developing Social Skills and Co-operation*. London: RoutledgeFalmer.

Brodie, I. (2003) *The Involvement of Parents and Carers in Sure Start Local Evaluations*. http//www.ness.bbk.ac.uk/HtmlDocuments/ParentInvolvmentGuidance2003.htm (accessed 23 September 2003).

Bruner, J. (1976) Functions of play, in J. Bruner (ed.) *On Knowing: Essays for the Left Hand*. New York: Atheneum.

Burt, C. (1921) *Mental and Scholastic Tests*. London: R.S. King and Son.

CACE (Central Advisory Council for Education) (1967) *Children and their Primary Schools (The Plowden Report)*. London: HMSO.

Clark, A. and Moss, P. (2001) *Listening to Young Children: The Mosaic Approach*. London: National Children's Bureau.

Cleave, S. and Sharp, C. (1986) *The Arts: A Preparation to Teach*. Slough: National Foundation for Educational Research.

Clegg, A. (1980) *About Our Schools*. London: Blackwell.

Clement, R. (1986) *The Art Teacher's Handbook*. London: Hutchinson.

Clement, R. (1993) *The Readiness of Primary School to Teach the National Curriculum Art*. Plymouth: Rolle Faculty of Arts Education, University of Plymouth.

Cooke, G., Griffin, D. and Cox, M. (1998) *Teaching Young Children to Draw*. London: The Falmer Press.

Cox, M. (1991) *The Child's Point of View*. Hemel Hempstead: Harvester, Wheatsheaf.

Cox, M. (1992) *Children's Drawings*. Harmondsworth: Penguin.

Cox, M.V. (1993) *Children's Drawings of the Human Figure*. Hove: Lawrence Erlbaum.

Cox, M. (1997) *Drawings of People by the Under–5s*. London: The Falmer Press.

Csiksentmihalyi, M.T. (1979) The concept of flow in play, in B. Sutton-Smith (ed.) *Play and Learning*. New York: Gardner Press.

Davies, B. (1989) *Frogs and Tails and Feminist Tales*. London: Allen and Unwin.

Davis, J. and Gardner, H. (1992) The cognitive revolution: consequences for the understanding and education of the child as artist, in B. Reimer and R.A. Smith (eds) *The Arts, Education and Aesthetic Knowing: Ninety-first Yearbook of the National Society for the Study of Education* (Part II, pp. 92–123). Chicago: University of Chicago Press.

Department of Health (1989) *The Children Act*. London: HMSO.

DfEE/SCAA (Department for Education and Employment/School Curriculum and Assessment Authority) (1996) *Desirable Outcomes for Children's Learning on Entering Compulsory Education*. London: DfEE/SCAA

Drummond, M.J. (1998) Another way of seeing: perceptions of play in a Steiner kindergarten. Paper presented at British Educational Research Association Conference, Belfast, 27–30 August.

Dyson, A.H. (1986) Transitions and tensions: interrelationships between the drawing, talking and dictating of young children, *Research Into the Teaching of English*, 24(4): 379–409.

Dyson, A.H. (1989) *Multiple Worlds of Child Writers: Friends Learning to Write*. New York: Teachers' College Press.

Dyson, A.H. (1993a) From prop to mediator: the changing role of written language in children's symbolic repertoires, in B. Spodek and O.N. Saracho (eds) *Year Book in Early Childhood Education. Language and Literacy in Early Childhood Education*, 4: 21–41. New York: Teachers' College Press.

Dyson, A.H. (1993b) *Social Worlds of Children Learning to Write in an Urban Primary School*. New York: Teachers' College Press.

Dweck, C.S. (1986) Motivational processes affecting meaning, *American Psychologist*, 41: 1030–48.

Dweck, C.S. (1991) Self theories and goals: their role in motivation, personality and development, in R. Deinstbeir (ed.) *Nebraska Symposium on Motivation, 1990*, 36: 199–235. Lincoln, NE: University of Nebraska Press.

Edwards, C., Gandini, L. and Forman, G. (eds) (1993) *The Hundred Languages of Children. The Reggio Emilia Approach to Early Childhood Education.* Norwood NJ: Ablex.

Egan, K. (1988) *Primary Understanding: Education in Early Childhood.* London: Routledge.

Egan, K. (1989) *Teaching as Story Telling: An Alternative Approach to Teaching and Curriculum in Elementary School.* Chicago: University of Chicago Press.

Eisner, E.W. (1972) *Educating Artistic Vision.* New York: Macmillan.

Fein, S. (1984) *Heidi's Horse.* Pleasant Hill, CA: Exelrod Press.

Freeman, N. (1980) *Strategies of Representation in Young Children.* London: Academic Press.

Gallas, K. (1994) *The Languages of Learning: How Children Talk, Write, Dance, Draw and Sing their Understanding of the World.* New York: Teachers' College Press.

Gardner, H. (1980) *Artful Scribbles.* New York: Basic Books.

Gentle, K. (1978) *Learning through Drawing.* Bradford: Art Galleries and Museums for the North Eastern Region of the Association for Advisers in Art and Design.

Golomb, C. (1981) Representation and reality: the origins and determinants of young children's drawings, *Review of Research in Visual Arts Education*, 14: 36–48.

Golomb, C. (1992) *The Child's Creation of a Pictorial World.* Berkley, CA: University of California Press.

Goodenough, F. (1926) *Measurement of Intelligence by Drawings.* New York: World Books.

Goodman, N. (1976) *Languages of Art.* Indianapolis: Hackett.

Gregory, E. (ed.) (1997) *One Child, Many Worlds: Early Learning in Multi-cultural Communities.* London: David Fulton.

Grieg, A. and Taylor, J. (1999) *Doing Research with Children.* London: Sage.

Hall, N. (1987) *The Emergence of Literacy.* Sevenoaks: Hodder and Stoughton.

Hamblin, K.A. (2002) Children's contextual art knowledge: local art and school art context comparisons, in L. Bresler and C.M. Thompson (eds) *The Arts in Children's Lives.* Dordrecht: Kluwer Academic.

Holland, P. (2000) Take the toys from the boys? An examination of the genesis of policy and appropriateness of adult perspectives in the area of war, weapon and superhero play, *Children's Social and Economic Education*, 4(2): 92–108.

Jones, E. (2001) Trying to break bad habits in practice by engaging with post-structuralist theories, *Early Years: An International Journal of Research and Development*, 21(1): 25–32.

Kellogg, R. (1969) *Analysing Children's Art*. Palo Alto, CA: Mayfield.

Kress, G. (1997) *Before Writing: Rethinking the Paths to Literacy*. London: Routledge.

Lave, J. and Wenger, E. (1991) *Situated Learning: Legitimate Peripheral Participation*. Cambridge: Cambridge University Press.

Lewis, A. and Lindsay, G. (eds) (2000) *Researching Children's Perspectives*. Buckingham: Open University Press.

Lindqvist, G. (2001) When small children play: how adults dramatise and children create meaning, *Early Years*, 21(1): 7–14.

Lowenfeld, V. (1947) *Creative and Mental Growth*. New York: Macmillan.

Lowenfeld, V. and Brittain, W. (1982) *Creative and Mental Growth*, 7th edn. New York: Macmillan.

Lucquet, G. (1913) *Les Dessins d'un Enfant*. Paris: Librairie Felix Alcan.

Lucquet, G. (1923) *Le Dessin Enfantin*. Paris: Delachaux et Niestle.

MacNaughton, G. (2000) *Rethinking Gender in Early Childhood Education*. St Leonard's, New South Wales: Allen and Unwin.

Malchiodi, C.A. (1998) *Understanding Children's Drawings*. New York: The Guildford Press.

Marsh, J. (2001) Parental involvement in literacy development: using media texts. Paper presented at British Educational Research Association Conference, Leeds, 12–15 September.

Marsh, J. (2002) The sound of silence: emergent technoliteracies and the early learning goals. Paper presented at British Educational Research Association Conference, Exeter, 12–14 September.

Marsh, J. and Millard E. (2000) *Literacy and Popular Culture: Using Children's Culture in the Classroom*. London: Paul Chapman.

Martin, B. Jr (Author) and Carle, E. (Illustrator) (1999) *Brown Bear, Brown Bear, What Do You See?*: Pearson Schools.

Matthews, J. (1994) *Helping Young Children to Paint and Draw: Children and Visual Representation*. London: Hodder and Stoughton.

Matthews, J. (1997) How young children learn to draw the human figure: Studies from Singapore, *European Early Education Research Journal*, Spring, pp. 29–58.

Matthews, J. (1999) *The Art of Childhood and Adolescence: The Construction of Meaning*. London: Falmer Press.

Matthews, J. (2001) Visual literacy: let children act naturally, *Five to Seven*, 1(4): 27–34.

Matthews, J. (2003) *Drawing and Painting: Children and Visual Representation*, 2nd edn. London: Paul Chapman.

Meadows, S. and Cashdan, A. (1983) Teaching styles in nursery education. Unpublished Final report to SSRC, London.

Morgan, M. (1988) *Art 4–11: Art in the Early Years of Schooling*. Hemel Hempstead: Simon and Schuster.

Moyles, J., Adams, S. and Musgrove, A. (2002) SPEEL: study of pedagogical effectiveness in early learning, *Department for Education and Skills Research Report RR363*. London: DfES.

NACCCE (National Advisory Committee for Creative and Cultural Education) (2001) *All Our Futures: Creativity, Culture and Education*. London: Department for Education and Employment.

Oxenbury, H. (Illustrator) and Rosen, M. (Author) *We're Going on a Bear Hunt*: Little Simon.

Pahl, K. (1999) *Transformations: Meaning Making in Nursery Education*. Stoke-on-Trent: Trentham Books.

Pahl, K. (2001) Children using popular culture at home: artefacts, drawing, multimedia. Paper presented at British Educational Research Association Conference, Leeds, 12–15 September.

Pahl, K. (2002) Ephemera, mess and miscellaneous piles: texts and practices in families, *Journal of Early Childhood Literacy*, 2(2): 145–66.

Paley, V.S. (1986a) *Boys and Girls: Superheroes in the Doll Corner*. Chicago: University of Chicago Press.

Paley, V.S. (1986b) On listening to what the children say, *Harvard Educational Review*, 56: 122–30.

Perry, L. (1992) Towards a definition of drawing, in D. Thistlewood (ed.) *Drawing: Research and Development*. Harlow: Longman in association with National Society for Education in Art and Design.

Pollard, A. (1996) *The Social World of Children's Learning*. London: Cassell.

Prosser, J. (ed.) (1998) *Image-based Research: A Sourcebook for Qualitative Researchers*. London: Purcell-Gates.

QCA (Qualifications and Curriculum Authority) (2003) *Creativity: Find it, Promote it*. www.qca.org.uk

QCA/DfEE (Qualifications and Curriculum Authority/Department for Education and Employment) (2000a) *A Scheme of Work for Key Stages 1 and 2. Art and Design Teachers' Guide*. London: QCA.

QCA/DfEE (Qualifications and Curriculum Authority/Department for Education and Employment) (2000b) *Curriculum Guidance for the Foundation Stage*. London: QCA.

Read, H. (1943) *Education Through Art*. London: Faber and Faber.

Robinson, K. (1982) *The Gulbenkian Report. The Arts in Schools: Principles, Practice and Provision*. London: Calouste Gulbenkian Foundation.

Rodger, R. (1999) *Planning an Appropriate Curriculum for the Under Fives*. London: David Fulton.

Rogoff, B. (1990) *Apprenticeships in Thinking: Cognitive Development in Social Context*. New York: Oxford University Press.

Schaffer, H.R. (1992) Joint involvement episodes as contexts for cognitive development, in H. McCurk (ed.) *Childhood and Social Development: Contemporary Perspectives*. Hove: Lawrence Erlbaum.

Schaffer, H.R. (1996) Joint involvement episodes as a context for development, in H. Daniels (ed.) *An Introduction to Vygotsky*. London: Routledge.

Selfe, L. (1977) *Nadia: A Case of Extraordinary Drawing Ability in an Autistic Child*. New York: Academic Press.

Siraj-Blatchford, I. (2004) Quality teaching in the early years, in A. Anning, J. Cullen and M. Fleer (eds) *Early Childhood Education: Society and Culture*. London: Sage.

Siraj-Blatchford, I., Sylva, K., Muttock, S., Gilden, R. and Bell, D. (2002) Researching effective pedagogy in the early years, *Department of Education and Skills Report RR356*. London: DfES.

Skelton, C. and Hall, E. (2001) *The Development of Gender Roles in Young Children: A Review of Policy and Literature*. Manchester: Equal Opportunties Commission.

Sutton-Smith, B. (1979) *Play and Learning*. New York: Gardner Press.

Sylva, K. (1994) School influences on children's development, *Journal of Child Psychology and Psychiatry*, 35(1): 135–70.

Sylva, K., Roy, C. and Painter, M. (1980) *Childwatching at Playgroup and Nursery School*. London: Grant McIntyre.

Tanner, R. (1989) *What I Believe: Lectures and Other Writings*. Bath: Holborne Museum and Crafts Centre.

Tomlinson, R.D. (1947) *Children as Artists*. London: Penguin.

Trevarthen, C. (1995) Mother and baby – seeing artfully eye to eye, in R. Gregory, J. Harris, P. Heard and D. Rose (eds) *The Artful Eye*. Oxford: Oxford University Press.

United Nations (1989) *Conventions on the Rights of the Child*. New York: United Nations.

Viola, W. (1936) *Child Art and Frank Cizek*. Vienna: Austrian Junior Red Cross.

Vygotsky, L.S. (1987) *The Collected Works of L.S. Vygostky*. New York: Plenum Press.

Vygotsky, L.S. (1995) *Fantasi och Kreativitet I Barndomen* [Imagination and Creativity in Childhood]. Gothenburg: Daidalos.

Weinberger, J. (1996) *Literacy Goes to School: The Parents' Role in Young Children's Literacy Learning*. London: Paul Chapman.

Whitbread, D. and Leeder, L. (2003) Sequencing and differentiation in young children's drawing, *Early Years*, 23(2): 155–76.

Willats, J. (1977) How children learn to represent three-dimensional space in drawings, in G. Butterworth (ed.) *The Child's Representation of the World*. New York: Plenum.

Willats, J. (1995) An information processing approach to drawing development, in C. Lange-Kuettner and C.V. Thomas (eds) *Drawing and Looking: Theoretical Approaches to Pictorial Representation in Children*. London: Harvester and Wheatsheaf.

Wilson, B. (1985) The artistic Tower of Babel: inextricable links between culture and graphic development, *Visual Arts Research*, 11: 90–104.

Wilson, B. (1992) Primitivism, the avant-garde and the art of little children, in D. Thistlewood (ed.) *Drawing: Research and Development*. Harlow: Longman in association with National Society of Art and Design.

Wilson, B. and Ligtvoet, J. (1992) Across time and cultures: stylistic changes in the dawings of Dutch children, in D. Thistlewood (ed.) *Drawing: Research and Development*. Harlow: Longman in association with National Society of Art and Design.

Wilson, B. and Wilson, M. (1977) An iconoclastic view of the imagery sources in the drawings of young people, *Art Education*, 30(1): 4–12.

Index

OBSERVING HARRY
CHILD DEVELOPMENT AND LEARNING 2–5

Cath Arnold

This book is about Harry, a determined little boy, who is intrinsically motivated to explore his world from an early age. His parents and grandparents find him so fascinating that they keep a written and video diary of Harry's play from when he is 8 months to 5 years. The author offers theories about how children learn and applies the theories to the observations of Harry.

The book demonstrates how effectively Harry accesses each area of the curriculum through his interests. It shows how Harry develops coping strategies when the family experiences major changes. It also highlights the contribution made by Harry's parents and his early years educators to his early education. Much of what we learn about Harry's early learning can be applied to many other young children.

This book about one child's early development and learning will be of interest to all who are fascinated by how young children learn – nursery practitioners, early years teachers, parents, students and advisers.

Contents
Introduction – Background about the book and using observation to assess children's development and learning – Getting to know Harry and his family – Using theory to understand Harry's development and learning – Harry's physical development – Harry's personal, social and emotional development – Harry learns to communicate, to use language and to become literate – Harry's mathematical development – Harry's creative development – Harry gains knowledge and understanding of the world – Harry's story – Reflections and making connections – References – Index.

160pp   0 335 21301 4 (Paperback)   0 335 21302 2 (Hardback)

SUPPORTING CREATIVITY AND IMAGINATION IN THE EARLY YEARS

Bernadette Duffy

This book draws on the author's experience of promoting young children's creativity and imagination in a variety of settings over the last twenty years. The settings include home and centre based care and this book draws on the practical experience of adults living and working with children in these settings. The aim of the book is to use real life examples of young children's development and their growing competence to show the richness of their creativity and imagination. Children's development across a wide range of creative and imaginative experiences are outlined and ways of planning and assessing children's progress are discussed. Insights from research are used to inform practice.

This book is for all who take delight in the richness of young children's learning and want to find ways to extend their practice by supporting and promoting learning in a practical way.

Contents
Acknowledgements – Series preface – Introduction – Part one: What are creativity and imagination and why are they important? – The importance of creativity and imagination for society and young children – Defining creativity and imagination – Creative and imaginative areas of experience – Part two: How do creativity and imagination develop? – The development of creativity and imagination from birth to 6 years – The creative process – Part three: Theory into practice – The role of the adult – The organization of space, time and social contexts – Widening children's experiences – Planning, implementing, observing, recording and assessing – Conclusion – References –Index.

176pp   0 335 19871 6 (Paperback)   0 335 19872 4 (Hardback)

CREATIVE CHILDREN, IMAGINATIVE TEACHING

Florence Beetlestone

- What does creativity mean in theory and in practice?
- Can all children and teachers respond creatively?
- What sorts of strategies can we adopt to promote a creative approach?

Creativity is a term often discussed in relation to education, particularly in primary schools. This book sets out to explore what it means in both practical and theoretical terms for children, teachers and the context in which they work. The key areas of planning, resourcing, organizing, managing and assessing creativity are dealt with in an accessible and readable style. Cameos and classroom examples are used in order to indicate effective strategies for promoting creativity within and across curriculum subjects. Creativity is shown to be a powerful force which can be harnessed to increase the learning potential of both teachers and children.

Contents
Introduction – Creativity and learning – Creativity and equal opportunities – Creative processes and products – Creativity and imagination – Creativity and originality – Creativity and nature – References – Index.

176pp   0 335 19783 3 (Paperback)   0 335 19784 1 (Hardback)